EARLY MONASTIC RULES

EARLY MONASTIC RULES

The RULES OF The FATHERS AND The REGULA ORIENTALIS

Translated by

Carmela Vircillo Franklin
Ivan Havener, O.S.B.
J. Alcuin Francis, O.S.B.

THE LITURGICAL PRESS
Collegeville, Minnesota

FRONT COVER: The opening of the *Regula Sanctorum Patrum Sarapionis, Macharii, Pafnutii, et Alterius Macharii*.
BACK COVER: The opening of the *Regula Macharii*.
From a 12th–13th century manuscript of monastic rules from the monastery of Admont. Reproduced with permission from Admont. Stiftsbibliothek Ms. 331, f.57r and f.59r, from a microfilm on deposit at the Hill Monastic Manuscript Library, St. John's University, Collegeville, Minnesota.

βX
2436
. Ɛ24

THE LITURGICAL PRESS
Collegeville, Minnesota 56321

Nihil obstat: Joseph C. Kremer, S.T.D., *Censor deputatus*.
Imprimatur: ✝ George H. Speltz, D.D., Bishop of St. Cloud. December 2, 1981.

Library of Congress Cataloging in Publication Data

Main Entry under title:

Early monastic rules.

Latin text with English translation.
Bibliography: p.
Contents: Rule of the Holy Fathers Serapion, Macarius, Paphnutius, and another Macarius — The Second Rule of the fathers — The Third Rule of the fathers — The Rule of Macarius — [etc.]
   1. Monasticism and religious orders—Rules. 2. Monasticism and religious orders—Early church, ca. 30–600. I. Franklin, Carmela Vircillo. II. Havener, Ivan, 1943–   III. Francis, J. Alcuin.
BX2436.E24   255   82-51
ISBN 0-8146-1251-2 (pbk.)   AACR2

CONTENTS

PREFACE

The decision to translate these early monastic rules was made at the first 1979–80 meeting of The Medieval Group at Saint John's University during the sesquimillennial celebration of the birth of Saint Benedict of Nursia. It was felt that making these rules available in English could be valuable for a general, non-specialist audience wishing to become familiar with the tradition that produced the Rule of St. Benedict. These translations are the result of that resolution.

Of the rules translated here, the Third Rule of the Fathers (3RP), the Rule of Macarius (RMac) and the *Regula Orientalis* (RO) have never been translated into English before. There are two primitive recensions of the Rule of the Four Fathers (RIVP): one, the Π recension, has been translated along with the Second Rule of the Fathers (2RP) (A Monk of Mount Saviour, "The Rule of Four Fathers" and "The Second Rule of the Fathers," revised and annotated by Adalbert de Vogüé, *Monastic Studies* 12 (1976) 249–263); the translation of the other, older recension, E, appears here for the first time. There is also an Italian translation of the Π recension of RIVP and of 2RP in Giuseppe Turbessi, *Regole monastiche antiche* (Rome: Edizioni Studium, 1974), pp. 317–334, and a French translation of all these rules in Vincent Desprez, *Règles monastiques d'Occident, IVᵉ–VIᵉ siècle* (Bégrolles-en-Mauges [Maine-et-Loire]: Abbaye de Bellefontaine, 1980).

We decided to include the Latin texts for handy reference, since they are scattered in various journals, and we have standardized the orthography. The most recent critical edition of the texts of the RIVP and 2RP is Jean Neufville, "Règle des IV Pères et Seconde Règle des Pères," *Revue Bénédictine* 77 (1967) 47–95. The critical text of RMac is found in Helga Styblo, "Die *Regula Macharii*," *Wiener Studien* 76 (1963) 124–150. For the RO, see Adalbert de Vogüé, "La *Regula Orientalis*. Texte critique et synopse des sources," *Benedictina* 13:2 (1976) 241–271. There is

7

as yet no modern critical edition of the 3RP; therefore, we have used the text of Migne, PL 103, cols. 443–446, taking into account, as well, the witness of two important manuscripts whose different readings are contained in the notes to Desprez' translation.

We have tried, in our translation, to remain as faithful to the Latin text as possible. Our purpose has been to present to the English reader these rules as historical documents rather than polished literary products. We have not supplied any critical apparatus but refer our readers to the critical editions of the Latin texts. We have included, however, references to Scripture, to the Rule of Benedict, and to the rules translated here, together with minimal footnotes.

We wish to thank the editors of the texts we have used and the publications in which they appear for their kind permission to reprint the Latin texts. Our work is based on their earlier research. We are grateful in particular to Adalbert de Vogüé, Giles Constable, and Bennett D. Hill for their generous suggestions.

At Saint John's, we wish to thank Abbot Jerome Theisen, O.S.B., and Father Michael Blecker, O.S.B., President of the University, who encouraged the publication of these rules. We also thank the Hill Monastic Manuscript Library, its director, Dr. Julian G. Plante, and its staff for helpful suggestions and for providing materials and a quiet place where some of this work was undertaken.

INTRODUCTION

Of the early monastic rules translated here, the first four —
the *Regulae Patrum*, or Rules of the Fathers (RIVP, 2RP, Rmac,
3RP) — form a clearly recognizable family. They belong to the
same lineage, each engendering the other in succession. With
the exception of Rmac, three of these — RIVP, 2RP, and 3RP —
also belong together in form; they are presented as deliberations
of abbatial synods. The close relationship of these four rules was
already recognized by Benedict of Aniane (750–812), who
grouped them together as part of his collection of monastic
rules, the *Codex regularum*.[1] Although the *Regula Orientalis* (RO)
does not share to the same extent in the interrelations within
this tightly knit group, it too belongs together with them, since
its author relies, in part, on 2RP as well as on the Rule of Pachomius.

The Rule of the Four Fathers (RIVP) is the oldest of the rules
included here. It belongs to the second generation of monastic
rules in the West, which followed the mother-rules of Pachomius, Basil and Augustine. Like the 2RP and the 3RP, it is presented as the minutes of a meeting of abbots. This is not a
literary convention. These rules are the deliberations of real
gatherings of superiors in charge of communities in the process
of developing the cenobitic life. The purpose of these abbatial
synods was not to provide complete monastic rules, but rather
to frame partial regulations, directed by immediate experience
and necessity.

The authors of these rules were most likely the secretaries of
the synods, who wrote down the words of the speakers.[2] In the
case of the RIVP, for instance, the names assigned to the speak-

---

[1] See Adalbert de Vogüé, "The Cenobitic Rules of the West," *Cistercian Studies*
12 (1977) 175–183, which classifies the monastic rules created before the end of
the eighth century; and Jean Neufville, "Règle des IV Pères et Seconde Règle
des Pères," *Revue Bénédictine* 77 (1967) 47–48.
[2] Ansgar Mundó, "Les anciens synodes abbatiaux et les *Regulae SS. Patrum*,"
Studia Anselmiana 44 (1959) 107–125; Neufville, pp. 48–49.

ers, the "Four Fathers" Serapion, Macarius, Paphnutius and the other Macarius, have been recognized as pseudonyms assigned by the first secretary to those who took the floor. Serapion, Paphnutius and the two Macarii are authentic Desert Fathers from Egypt who appear in the literature of desert monasticism — the *Apophthegmata* (*The Sayings of the Desert Fathers*), Palladius' *Historia Lausiaca* (*Lausiac History*), and Rufinus' *Historia monachorum in Aegypto* (*History of the Monks of Egypt*). Although contemporary with one another, these four anchoritic Fathers probably never met, let alone wrote — in Latin — a rule for cenobitic monks.[3]

There are three current views on the place and date of origin of RIVP. Some have suggested that the RIVP was composed during the second half of the fifth century in southern Gaul, in Provence or Narbonne, perhaps under the influence of Lérins, one of the most flourishing centers of Latin monasticism at that time.[4] Others prefer Italy, and specifically the neighborhood of Rome, during the second quarter or middle of the fifth century.[5] Most recently, Lérins, but between 400 and 410, has been put forth as the monastic community associated with RIVP. [6]

Two very old recensions of RIVP exist. The so-called E recension, translated here, seems to be the original one. It has survived in many manuscripts, an indication of its influence and popularity. The other recension, Π, is found in only one manuscript, dating from the beginning of the seventh century. Although very old, it is already a reworked and polished version of the original rule.[7]

---

[3] Neufville, pp. 48–49, n. 7. Furthermore, it has been suggested that only three Fathers spoke. "Macarius" spoke twice, and later scribes thought of two Macarii, because of the two famous historical Macarii, Macarius of Egypt and Macarius of Alexandria. Giuseppe Turbessi, *Regole monastiche antiche* (Rome: Edizioni Studium, 1974), p. 320.

[4] Mundó, p. 117.

[5] Neufville, pp. 61ff.

[6] This is de Vogüé's opinion, cited and supported in Vincent Desprez, *Règles monastiques d'Occident* (Bégrolles-en-Mauges [Maine-et-Loire]: Abbaye de Bellefontaine, 1980), pp. 91–92.

[7] Neufville, pp. 53–61. Jean Neufville, "Sur le texte de la Règle des IV Pères," *Revue Bénédictine* 75 (1965) 307–312 and "Les éditeurs des *Regulae Patrum*," *Revue Bénédictine* 76 (1966) 327–343 discuss the textual history of RIVP, with remarks on 2RP as well.

While the RIVP has tenuous links to Augustine, Pachomius, and Basil, there are, however, no clear and obvious borrowings from these first monastic legislators. Despite the "Egyptian orientation," emphasized by the names given to the Four Fathers, this influence was hardly direct. Rather, it can be explained by the long-established presence in Rome and in the West of Egyptian pilgrim-monks since the time of Athanasius' visit to the See of Rome (340–341), when Antony and Pachomius were still alive.[8]

The Second Rule of the Fathers (2RP) is closely dependent on RIVP. It seems to have been written to provide guidance in some areas not dealt with by RIVP, especially concerning the interior life of the monks.[9] As is the case for its mother-rule, there are three opinions concerning its place and date of origin: Italy, in the years between 450 and 475;[10] or the same region of Provence and Narbonne that engendered RIVP, at the end of the fifth century;[11] or Lérins, around 427.[12]

Despite its brevity, 2RP exercised considerable influence, beginning immediately with the Rule of Macarius (RMac), which often repeats passages from 2RP word for word. The Macarius of its title is Macarius the Alexandrian († ca. 394), who lived as a hermit in the desert of Skete and Nitria and whose ascetic exploits have been transmitted by the literature of the Desert Fathers. However, it is generally recognized that the hermit Macarius could not have been the author of a cenobitic, Latin rule and that this document could not have been composed in the desert of northwestern Egypt. Rather, it is very likely that the RMac was written in Provence, possibly in the region under the influence of Lérins, since John of Réome († ca. 545) used it on his return from Lérins to reform his monastery of Moutiers-Saint-Jean.

The dating of RMac is controversial, since it depends on the dating of the earlier 2RP. The last decades of the fifth century have most frequently been suggested. Its unknown author, writing in Latin but under the influence of Egyptian monasti-

---

[8] Neufville, "Règle," pp. 66–68.
[9] Ibid., p. 50, and n. 2.
[10] Mundó, p. 118.
[11] Neufville, "Règle," pp. 61ff.
[12] Desprez, pp. 91–92.

cism, gave his rule the title *Regula Macharii* to attract attention to it and invest it with authority, much like the secretary who appropriated the names of the Four Fathers for his rule.[13]

The Third Rule of the Fathers (3RP) belongs to the next generation of monastic legislators. Like RIVP and 2RP, the fourteen short chapters of this rule consist of the minutes of a gathering of monastic superiors. However, it does not borrow directly from RIVP or 2RP, but from the RMac, as well as from several Gallic councils. It was composed in Gaul, in the first half of the sixth century. It still awaits a modern critical edition.[14]

Contemporary with the RMac is the *Regula Orientalis* (RO), which has been dated to the last decades of the fifth century.[15] Its place of origin has been more difficult to localize. Italy and Provence have been offered as possibilities, although most recently the theory has been set forth that it originated in the monastery of Condat, in the French Jura region, under the influence of Lérins.[16] The attribution of authorship of the RO to a certain Vigilius the Deacon does not have any historical basis.[17]

The RO is a patchwork of literal borrowings from the Rule of Pachomius, free citations from 2RP, and original material from the anonymous redactor. The Pachomian material is grouped in two large sections of the RO, chapters 4–23 and 36–47. Both sections reproduce the exact order of the Pachomian text. One quarter of Pachomius' rule is quoted and a slightly larger fraction of the shorter 2RP.[18]

---

[13] Helga Styblo, "Die *Regula Macharii*," *Wiener Studien* 76 (1963) pp. 126ff.; Desprez, pp. 140–141.

[14] Mundó, p. 35. A. de Vogüé, whose text of 3RP, as well as RIVP (both E and II recensions), 2RP, RMac, and RO, will be published next year in *Sources chrétiennes*, very kindly informed us by letter that the latest results of his investigation on 3RP show that it was the product of the Council of Clermont in 535. We await with interest the details of his discoveries in the forthcoming publication.

[15] This dating is determined by references to the RO in *The Life of the Fathers of the Jura*. See A. de Vogüé, "La *Vie des Pères du Jura* et la datation de la *Regula Orientalis*," *Revue d'ascétique et de mystique* 47 (1971) 121–127.

[16] A. de Vogüé, "La *Regula Orientalis*. Texte critique et synopse des sources," *Benedictina* 13:2 (1976) 241–271. De Vogüé has put forth this latest suggestion. See Desprez, p. 117.

[17] It was the RO's seventeenth-century editor, Lukas Holste, who ascribed it to Vigilius; this assumption was followed by all later editors. De Vogüé, "La *Regula Orientalis*," p. 242.

[18] Ibid., pp. 242–245.

All the rules included here would, by comparison with later rules, be called fragmentary. The Rules of the Fathers complement one another, each legislating in areas not addressed by the others or modifying an earlier precept. In the RMac, there are no extensive prescriptions for the order of prayer. Nothing is said about how the monks should sleep or what they should wear. Although the RO reflects a much more complex monastic organization and encompasses almost all facets of monastic observance, it still remains a series of injunctions strung together without a guiding plan.

Yet, these rules illustrate for the student of monasticism the early development of the cenobitic life in the West, from its infancy with RIVP to the time of Benedict, whose rule is contemporary with the 3RP. The RIVP, only one generation away from the mother-rules of Pachomius, Basil, and Augustine, portrays a form of monastic life just emerging from the hermitage. It is the problems connected with the formation of cenobitic communities that this earliest rule addresses.[19] In contrast, the RO and 3RP reflect the great organizational development that has occurred in one century. In the RO, for example, we find discussion of the role of the abbot, the prior, cellarer, and correction of faults that is very close to the Rule of Benedict (RB).[20]

The evolution of cenobitic life illustrated in these rules can be followed most clearly in the development of monastic terminology reflecting the increasing complexity and specialization of monastic organization. This is most strikingly documented in our rules by the terms used to indicate the superior of the monastery. In the Rule of Pachomius as translated by Jerome, the head of the monastery is called the *pater monasterii* ("father of the monastery") or *princeps* ("prince, head").[21] *Is qui praeest* ("he who presides") is the term used in Basil as well as in RIVP and 2RP. In 2RP, however, we see, as well, a new term, *praepositus*, used to address the superior. This term is also used in the later II recension of RIVP.[22] In the RO and RMac, as well as in the contemporary rules of the Master and Caesarius of Arles, the

---

[19] Neufville, "Règle," pp. 62ff.
[20] De Vogüé, "La *Regula Orientalis*," p. 241.
[21] These terms are kept in the sections of the RO borrowed from Pachomius.
[22] This is one principal reason for II's later dating. Neufville, "Règle," p. 48.

word *abbas* ("abbot") to refer to the superior is introduced, and the word *praepositus* has acquired the new meaning of the second in command. This distinction, however, is not always maintained yet. In chapter 7 of RMac, for example, the word *praepositus* probably still refers to the head of the monastery. No such confusion arises in 3RP, contemporary with the RB; here the abbot is always referred to as *abbas*, and the *praepositus* is clearly the abbot's lieutenant, Benedict's prior.

The influence of some of these rules on the RB has already been recognized; the possible influence of others, however, has not yet been studied.[23] These rules illustrate once again that the most striking characteristic of early monastic literature was a very extensive and increasingly complex network of borrowing from each other. At the same time, in combination with this conservative trend, one witnesses here the great progression of cenobitic monasticism in the century immediately before Benedict.

---

[23] *RB 1980: The Rule of St. Benedict in Latin and English with Notes* (Collegeville, Minn.: The Liturgical Press, 1981), pp. 87ff., for example, recognizes that Benedict was acquainted with RIVP and 2RP. Yet nothing is said here of RMac, although parallels with RB are listed in the Index, p. 599.

ABBREVIATIONS

RIVP	Rule of the Four Fathers
2RP	Second Rule of the Fathers
3RP	Third Rule of the Fathers
RMac	Rule of Macarius
RO	*Regula Orientalis*
RB	Rule of Benedict

INCIPIT REGULA SANCTORUM PATRUM SARAPIONIS, MACHARII, PAFNUTII ET ALTERIUS MACHARII

[I] [1] Sedentibus nobis in unum, [2] consilio saluberrimo comperti Dominum nostrum rogavimus ut nobis *tribueret Spiritum Sanctum* [3] *qui* nos *instrueret* qualiter fratrum conversationem vel regulam vitae ordinare possimus.

[II] Sarapion dixit [1] quoniam *misericordia Domini plena est terra* et multorum agmina ad vitae fastigium tendent [2] et quia heremi vastitas et diversorum monstrorum terror singillatim habitare fratres non patitur. [3] Optimumque videtur Spiritus Sancti praeceptis oboedire, [4] nec nostra propria verba possunt firma perseverare nisi firmitas Scripturarum nostrum ordinem firmet. [5] Quae dicit: *Ecce quam bonum et quam iocundum habitare fratres in unum;* [6] et iterum: *Qui habitare facit unianimes in domo.* [7] Firma iam nunc regula pietatis per Spiritus Sancti ostensionem praeclaram, fratrum regulam ordinare prosequamur.

[III] [8] Volumus ergo *fratres unianimes in domo cum iocunditate habitare;* [9] sed qualiter unianimitas ipsa vel iocunditas recto ordine teneatur Deo iuvante mandamus.

Pr.0 Following Neufville's suggestion ("Règle," p. 71) the text of the RIVP is divided into four speeches, each one ascribed to a different father, and has a preface at the beginning as well as an appendix at the end. The chapter divisions [in brackets] correspond to those in the Migne text of Benedict of Aniane's *Codex regularum* (PL 103, cols. 435–442). References to the RIVP, however, are cited according to the speech divisions suggested by Neufville.
Pr.3 "manner" (*conversationem*): the term frequently appears in RO and RB, e.g., RO 1.1, 7; RB 58.17, etc.
"rule of the life" (*regulam vitae*): here "rule" has the older, non-technical sense of a "norm of conduct."
"brothers" (*fratrum*): this is the designation for monastic members in this rule, whereas "monks" (*monachi*) does not appear at all.
1.0 This first section records the transition from an eremitical to a cenobitic way of life; Neufville, "Règle," p. 62.
1.1 The RIVP cites Psalms according to the Roman Psalter.
1.3 Cf. Josh 24:24.
1.7 "guide to piety" (*regula pietatis*): this same expression occurs again in RIVP

RULE OF THE HOLY FATHERS
SERAPION, MACARIUS, PAPHNUTIUS
AND ANOTHER MACARIUS

Preface

[Chapter 1]

[1] While we were sitting together, [2] seeking knowledge from a most beneficial deliberation, we asked our Lord that *he bestow* on us *the Holy Spirit* [3] *who might instruct* (Gal 3:5; 1 Cor 2:16) us how we ought to determine the manner and rule of the life of the brothers.

1. Essence of Cenobitism

[Chapter 2]

Serapion said [1] that *the earth is filled with the mercy of the Lord* (Ps 32[33]:5) and bands of many men strive for the summit of life [2] and that the desolation of the desert and the terror of various monsters do not permit the brothers to live singly. [3] And it seems best to obey the precepts of the Holy Spirit, [4] nor are our own words able to remain weighty unless the power of Scripture strengthens our regulation. [5] It says, *Behold how good and pleasant it is that brothers live together* (Ps 132[133]:1), [6] and again, *He who makes men live harmoniously in a house* (Ps 67[68]:7). [7] Now with this powerful guide to piety through the very clear manifestation of the Holy Spirit, let us proceed to lay down a rule for the brothers.

[Chapter 3]

[8] Therefore we desire that the *brothers live harmoniously in a house pleasantly* (Ps 67[68]:7 + Ps 132[133]:9); [9] but with God's help let us legislate how that harmony and pleasantness be maintained in proper order.

4.2 and has the non-technical meaning of *regula. Pietas* is a virtue.

"rule for the brothers" (*fratrum regulam*): here *regula* has the newer, technical sense of a "monastic rule."

[IV] [10] Volumus ergo unum praeesse super omnes, [11] nec ab eius consilio vel imperio quicquam sinistrum declinare, [12] sed sicut imperio Domini cum omni laetitia oboedire, [13] dicente Apostolo ad Hebreos: *Oboedite praepositis vestris, quia ipsi vigilant pro vobis;* [14] et Dominus dixit: *Nolo sacrificium, sed oboedientiam.*
[15] Considerandum est quoque ab his qui se tali opere unianimes esse cupiunt quia per oboedientiam *Abraham placuit Deo et amicus Dei appellatus est.* [16] Per oboedientiam ipsi apostoli meruerunt *testes* Domino *in tribubus et populis esse.* [17] Ipse quoque Dominus noster *de superna ad inferiora discendens* ait: *Non veni facere voluntatem meam sed eius qui me misit.*
[18] His ergo tantis virtutibus firmata oboedientia magnopere, magno studio teneatur.

[V] Macharius dixit [1] quoniam fratrum insignia virtutum habitationis vel oboedientiae superius conscripta sunt. [2] Nunc qualiter spiritale exercitium ab his qui praesunt teneatur Deo iuvante ostendimus.

[3] Debet is qui praeest talem se exhibere ut Apostolus ait: *Estote forma credentibus;* [4] hoc est, pro qualitate misticae pietatis et veritatis fratrum *animas* ad caelestia de terrenis *erigere,* [5] dicente Apostolo: *Argue, obsecra, increpa cum omni lenitate;* [6] et alio loco inquit: *Quid vultis? in virga veniam ad vos an in spiritu mansuetudinis?*

[7] Decernendum est ab illo qui praeest qualiter circa singulos

---

1.10 "one preside over all" (*unum praeesse super omnes*): this phrase designates the major superior in the RIVP (usually "he who presides" [*is qui praeest*]). It is an archaic expression also found in Rufinus' translation of Basil's Rule, 15, but there is no evidence that the RIVP borrows directly from Basil. The word "abbot" (*abbas*) does not appear in this rule.
1.13 "superiors" (*praepositis*): appearing in a scriptural quotation, this term does not have a technical meaning in RIVP. This scriptural passage is alluded to in RB 2.38.
1.15 "obedience" (*oboedientiam*): this is one of the key monastic virtues; cf. RB 58.17.
1.16 There may also be an allusion here to Matt 4:19-22; cf. RB 5.7-8.
1.17 John 6:38-39 is also quoted by RB 5.13.
2.4 "spiritual" (*misticae*): this word appears only here among the early monastic rules in the West.
2.5 This scriptural passage is also quoted by RB 2.23.
2.7 RB 2.23-24.

[Chapter 4]

[10] We desire that one preside over all, [11] that no one deviate perversely from his advice or command [12] but obey in all happiness, as though it were the command of the Lord; [13] as the Apostle says to the Hebrews, *Obey your superiors because they keep watch for you* (Heb 13:17), [14] and the Lord said, *I do not desire sacrifice but obedience* (1 Sam 15:22 [cf. Sir 4:17] + Matt 9:13 [cf. Hos 6:6]).

[15] Also, it ought to be considered by those who wish themselves to be in accord with such a work that through obedience *Abraham was pleasing to God and was called God's friend* (Jas 2:23 [cf. Gen 15:6; 1 Macc 2:52; Heb 11:8]). [16] By obedience the apostles themselves merited *to be witnesses* to the Lord *among tribes and peoples* (Acts 1:8 + Rev 11:3, 9). [17] Also our Lord himself, *descending from the upper to the lower regions*, says, *I have not come to do my will but that of him who sent me* (John 8:23 + Eph 4:9 [cf. Jas 1:17] + John 6:38-39).

[18] So let obedience, especially strengthened by such great virtues, be maintained with great care.

2. Role of the Superior
Reception of Postulants and Guests

[Chapter 5]

Macarius said [1] that the marks of the brothers' virtues—of their dwelling place and obedience—have already been prescribed. [2] Now we show with God's help how the spiritual discipline should be maintained by those who preside.

[3] He who presides should conduct himself just as the Apostle says, *Be a model to those who believe* (1 Thess 1:7), [4] that is, *to rouse the souls* (2 Macc 15:10 [cf. 1 Cor 15:47-49]) of the brothers from terrestrial to celestial matters by the quality of his spiritual piety and truth, [5] in accord with the Apostle who says, *Reprove, entreat, rebuke with all gentleness* (2 Tim 4:2); [6] and in another passage he says, *What do you want?—that I come to you with a rod, or in a spirit of meekness?* (1 Cor 4:21).

[7] It should be discerned by that one who presides how he ought to show the disposition of piety around individuals. [8] He

debeat pietatis affectum monstrare. [8] Aequalitatem tenere debet, [9] non immemor Domini dicentis: *In qua mensura mensi fueritis remitietur vobis.*

[VI] [10] Astantibus ergo ad orationem, nullus praesumat sine praecepto eius qui praeest psalmi laudem emittere. [11] Ordo iste teneatur ut nullus priorem in monasterio ad standum vel psallendi ordinem praesumat praecedere, [12] dicente Salomone: *Fili, primatum concupiscere noli;* [13] *neque adcubueris prior in convivio, ne veniat melior te et dicatur tibi: "Surge," et confusionem patiaris;* [14] et iterum dicit: *Noli altum sapere, sed time.* [15] Quod si tardat is qui praeest, oportet primum in notitiam eius deferre, et secundum imperium eius oboedire convenit.

[VII] [16] Qualiter vero examinatio erga eos qui de saeculo convertuntur teneri debeat ostendimus. [17] Amputandae sunt primo ab huiuscemodi divitiae saeculi.

[18] Quod si aliquis pauper converti videatur, habet et ipse divitias quas amputare debeat, [19] quas Spiritus Sanctus ostendit per Salomonem dicens: *Odit anima mea pauperem superbum;* [20] et alio loco dicit: *Sicut vulneratum superbum.* [21] Debet ergo is qui praeest magno studio hanc regulam tenere ut si pauper convertitur primo exponat sarcinam superbiae, [22] et sic examinatus suscipiatur. [23] Debet ante omnia humilitate imbui, ut quod magnum est et Deo sacrificium acceptum est suam voluntatem non faciat sed *ad omnia paratus* sit; [24] quidquid accederit memor esse debet: *In tribulatione patientes.* [25] Is qui talis est cum de saeculi latebras liberari voluerit, primum, adpropians monasterio, ebdomada pro foribus iaceat; [26] nullus cum eo de fratribus iun-

---

2.8 "equality" (*aequalitatem*): cf. RB 2.16-22 and RIVP 5.12-13.

2.10 RB 47.3.

2.11 RB 63.1-9 speaks of ordering according to time of entrance into the monastic community.

2.14 "it says" (*dicit*): this means that "Scripture says," but the context could inaccurately suggest that Solomon is still speaking: "he says." The Π text avoids the latter impression by introducing this Pauline text with "it is said" (*dicitur*).

2.18 Augustine also warns against the pride of the poor; see Augustine, *Praeceptum* I.4-6.

2.21 "rule" (*regulam*): here the term has the old meaning of "norm of conduct" or "law."

2.23 "humility" (*humilitate*): this is one of the key monastic virtues.

2.24 "patient" (*patientes*): this is another key monastic virtue.

2.25 Cf. Gal 1:4; RB 58.3 suggests a waiting period of four or five days.

ought to maintain equality, [9] not forgetful of the Lord who says, *By that measure you have measured, it will be measured to you again* (Matt 7:2).

[Chapter 6]

[10] Let no one among those assisting at prayer presume to utter the praise of a psalm without the command of him who presides. [11] That ordering is to be maintained, so that no one may presume to precede another of higher rank in the monastery for standing or for the order of the singing of the psalms, [12] in accord with Solomon who says, *Son, do not desire to seek the first place* (Sir 7:4 + Prov 25:6-7), [13] *nor should you recline at a banquet too early, lest someone greater than you come and it is said to you, "Get up!" and you suffer embarrassment* (Luke 14:8-9); [14] and again it says, *Do not wish to be extremely wise, but fear* (Rom 11:20). [15] But if he who presides delays, it is necessary first to bring it to his attention, and it is appropriate to obey according to his command.

[Chapter 7]

[16] Just how an examination of those who are converted from the world should be undertaken, we demonstrate. [17] The riches of the world ought first to be lopped off from such a one.

[18] If any poor man is seen to be converted, he, too, has riches which he should lop off, [19] which the Holy Spirit shows through Solomon, saying, *My soul hates a proud poor man* (Sir 25:3-4); [20] and in another passage he says, *the proud man, as one wounded* (Ps 88[89]:11). [21] Therefore, he who presides should hold this rule with great care, so that if a poor man is converted, let him first expose his heavy sack of pride [22] and, thus examined, let him be received. [23] He ought to be imbued with humility above all things so that he may not do his own will, which is a great sacrifice, acceptable to God, but be *prepared for all things* (2 Tim 2:21); [24] whatever happens, he must be mindful to be *patient in tribulation* (Rom 12:12). [25] Let such a one, when he desires to be freed from the recesses of the world, lie prostrate for a week before the gates when he first approaches the monastery; [26] let

2.26 RB 58.8.

gatur, nisi semper dura et laboriosa ei proponantur. [27] *Si vero
perseveraverit pulsans*, petenti non negetur ingressus, [28] sed is qui
praeest huiuscemodi hominem instruere debet qualiter vitam
fratrum vel regulam tenere possit.
[29] Quod si divis est habens multas divitias in saeculo et converti voluerit, debet primo Dei voluntatem implere [30] et conse-
qui praeceptum illum praecipuum quod adulescenti diviti dicitur: [31] *Vende omnia tua et da pauperibus, et tolle crucem tuam et
sequere me.* [32] Deinde instruendus est ab eo qui praeesse videtur
ut nihil sibi relinquat nisi crucem quam teneat et sequatur Dominum. [33] Crucis vero fastigia quae tenenda sunt: primum, omni
oboedientia non suam voluntatem facere sed alterius. [34] Quod si
voluerit monasterio partem conferre, noverit quo ordine sive
ipse sive eius oblatio suscipiatur. [35] Si autem voluerit de suis
servis secum habere, noverit *iam non* eum *servum* habere *sed
fratrem*, ut in omnibus perfectus inveniatur.

[VIII] [36] Qualiter   peregrini   hospites   suscipiantur.
[37] Venientibus eis nullus nisi unus cui cura fuerit iniuncta occur-
rat ut responsum det venienti. [38] Non licebit ei orare nec pacem
offerre, nisi primo videatur ab eo qui praeest, [39] et oratione
simul peracta sequatur ordinem suum pacis officium. [40] Nec
licebit alicui cum superveniente sermocinari nisi soli qui praeest
aut quos ipse voluerit. [41] Venientibus vero ad horam refectionis,
non licebit peregrino fratri cum fratribus manducare, nisi cum

---

2.27 RB 58.3-4.
2.28 "rule" (*regulam*): here the term has the technical meaning of "monastic rule."
2.31 Matt 16:24 is also quoted by RB 4.10.
2.33 "fulcrum of the cross" (*crucis vero fastigia*): this is the place where the full weight of the cross is to be borne.
2.34 Cf. RB 58.24.
2.35 "perfect" (*perfectus*): this is one of the goals of monastic life and is mentioned again in RIVP 4.12.
2.36 "travelers" (*peregrini hospites*): whether this refers to all guests who are passing through or only to traveling monastic brothers is unclear; see note on 2.41.
2.38 "offer the peace" (*pacem offerre*): this is a reference to the giving of the kiss of peace.
2.39 "rite of peace" (*pacis officium*): this is the actual rite of the kiss of peace; cf. RB 53.4-5.
2.40 Cf. RO 26.4; RB 53:23-24.

none of the brothers be associated with him, and only what is harsh and laborious ever be set before him. [27] Certainly *if he has persevered knocking* (Luke 11:8 [cf. Acts 12:16]), let entrance not be denied to him who seeks, [28] but he who presides ought to instruct such a man, how he can follow the life of the brothers and the rule.

[29] But if he is wealthy, having many riches in the world, and desires to be converted, he should first fulfill God's will [30] and follow that principal precept that is spoken to the rich young man, [31] *Sell all your goods and give to the poor, and take up your cross and follow me* (Matt 19:21 + 16:24). [32] Then he should be instructed by him who is seen to preside, that he keep nothing for himself except the cross of Christ which he should bear, and that he follow the Lord. [33] Certainly the fulcrum of the cross which ought to be borne is, first, in all obedience not to do his own will but another's. [34] But if he desire to bestow a portion on the monastery, he should know by what manner, whether he himself or his offering be received. [35] If he desires, however, to keep one of his slaves with him, he should know that he *no longer* possesses him *as a slave but as a brother* (Phlm 16 [cf. Matt 19:21]), so that in all things he might be found perfect.

[Chapter 8]

[36] How travelers should be received. [37] No one may meet those who come except the one to whom this care has been enjoined, that he receive him who comes. [38] It will not be permitted for him to pray or offer the peace unless he is first seen by him who presides; [39] and when prayer together has been concluded, let the rite of peace follow according to its order. [40] Nor will it be permitted for anyone to converse with one who comes, with the sole exception of him who presides or those whom he wishes. [41] But for those who come at mealtime, it will not be permitted for a traveling brother to eat with the brothers, unless

---

2.41 "traveling brother" (*peregrino fratri*): if "brother" refers only to a monastic member, as it does elsewhere in this rule, then the "travelers" of 2.36 may all be monastic; on the other hand, the monastic brother may be singled out from the travelers to show that even he is not treated differently than other guests who are passing through; cf. RB 56.1.

eo qui praeest, ut possit aedificari. [42] Nulli licebit loqui nec alicuius audiatur sermo nisi divinus qui ex pagina profertur, et
eius qui praeest, vel quibus ipse iusserit loqui ut aliquid de Deo
conveniat.

[IX] Pafnutius dixit: [1] Magna et utilia ad animae salutem
dicta sunt omnia. [2] Nec hoc tacendum est, qualiter ieiuniorum
ordo tenendus sit. [3] Nec aliud huic firmum testimonium convenit nisi in eo quod dicit: [4] *Petrus autem et Iohannes ascendebant in
templum circa horam orationis nonam.* [5] Debet ergo iste ordo teneri
ut nullo die nisi nona reficiatur in monasterio excepto dominica
die. [6] Die autem dominica non nisi Deo vacetur; [7] nulla operatio
in eo die comperiatur nisi tantum *hymnis et psalmis et canticis
spiritalibus* dies transigatur.

[X] [8] Qualiter debent fratres operari praecipimus. [9] Debet
ergo iste ordo teneri. [10] A prima hora usque ad tertiam Deo
vacetur. [11] A tertia vero usque ad nonam, quidquid iniunctum
fuerit sine aliqua murmuratione suscipiatur. [12] Meminere debent hi quibus iniungitur dictum Apostoli: *Omnia quae facitis sine
murmuratione facite.* [13] Timere debent illum dictum terribile: *Nolite murmurare sicut quidam eorum murmuraverunt et ab extermina-
tore perierunt.* [14] Debet etiam qui praeest opus quod faciendum
est uni iniungere ut ceteri eius praecepto cui iniunctum fuerit
oboediant.

2.42 RB 38:8-9.

3.1 Cf. 1 Pet 1:9.

3.2 "regulation of fasts" (*ieiuniorum ordo*): the regulation described here refers
to the monastic practice of waiting till None before eating.

3.6 At the time of the RIVP, this rule applied only to the monastic brothers.

3.8 "ought to be occupied" (*debent . . . operari*): this concerns the work of the
monastic brothers.

3.11 "murmuring" (*murmuratione*): grumbling is often attacked in the RB and
in other monastic rules, e.g., RB 5.17-19; 23.1; 34.6, etc.; Rufinus' translation of
Basil's Rule, 70.

3.13 This scriptural passage is alluded to in RB 5.19.

with him who presides, so that he may be edified. [42] It will be permitted for no one to speak, nor may the speech of anyone be heard unless it be of a spiritual nature, which is presented from the [sacred] page and [the talk] of him who presides or those he has commanded to speak, so that the topic be appropriately concerning God.

3. Fasting and Work

[Chapter 9]

Paphnutius said [1] that all things great and useful for the welfare of the soul have been spoken of. [2] Nor should this be passed over in silence, how the regulation of fasts ought to be maintained. [3] Not any other firm testimony is fitting for this, except in that [passage] which says, [4] *Moreover, Peter and John went up into the temple about the ninth hour of prayer* (Acts 3:1). [5] Therefore, that regulation ought to be maintained so that on any day only at the ninth hour may there be refreshment in the monastery, except on the Lord's Day. [6] On the Lord's Day, however, nothing is done except it be devoted to God; [7] no activity should take place on that day, with the sole exception that the day be spent *in hymns, psalms, and spiritual songs* (Eph 5:19).

[Chapter 10]

[8] We prescribe how the brothers ought to be occupied: [9] therefore, this order ought to be followed. [10] From the first hour to the third, this time should be devoted to God. [11] But from the third even to the ninth, let whatever has been enjoined be undertaken without any murmuring. [12] These to whom it is enjoined should be mindful of that saying of the Apostle, *Everything that you do, do without murmuring* (Phil 2:14). [13] They ought to fear that dreadful saying, *Desire not to murmur, as certain of them murmured and perished by extermination* (1 Cor 10:10). [14] Moreover, he who presides ought to enjoin on one the work which should be done so that the rest may obey the command of that one to whom it had been enjoined.

[XI] [15] Qualiter infirmitas vel possibilitas corporum ab eo qui praeest cognoscenda sit. [16] Si quis ex fratribus per ieiunia vel operam manuum—[17] quam Apostolus praecipit: *Operantes manibus nostris ne quem vestrum gravaremus*—[18] is qui talis est, si fuerit infirmitate obsessus, providendum est ab eo qui praeest qualiter ipsa infirmitas sustentetur. [19] Quod si infirmus est animo huiuscemodi frater, oportet eum frequentius operari, considerans Apostolum qualiter *corpus suum servituti redigit.* [20] Hoc autem observandum est ut in nullo voluntatem suam faciat.

[XII] [21] Qualiter officiis mutuis se fratres praeveniant. [22] Si fratrum congregatio multa est, debet is qui praeest ebdomadarum ordinem et officia quae sibi invicem succedant in ministrando decernere.

[23] Qualis debeat esse qui cellarium fratrum contineat. [24] Debet talis eligi qui possit in omnibus guilae suggestionibus dominari, [25] qui timeat Iudae sententiam qui *ab initio fur fuit.* [26] Studere debet qui huic officio deputatur ut audiat: [27] *Qui bene ministraverit bonum gradum sibi adquirit.*

[28] Nosse etiam debent fratres quia quidquid in monasterio tractatur sive in vasis sive in ferramentis vel cetera omnia esse sanctificata. [29] Si quis neglegenter aliquid tractaverit, [30] partem se habere noverit cum illo rege qui in vasis domus Dei sanctificatis cum suis bibebat concubinis et qualem meruit vindictam.

[31] Custodienda sunt ista praecepta et per singulos dies in aures fratrum recensenda.

3.16 "work of the hands" (*operam manuum*): cf. RB 48.8, "by the labor of their hands" (*labore manuum suarum*).

3.17 1 Cor 4:12 is quoted by RB 7.43 and alluded to in RB 4.32; 48.8.

3.19 This scriptural passage is also quoted by RB 2.13; 4.11.

3.21 "mutual duties" (*officiis mutuis*): cf. Rom 12:10; RB 63.17; 72.4, 7.

3.22 "community" (*congregatio*): this term appears frequently in the RB in the same sense, e.g., RB 3.1; 17.6, etc.

"order of the weekly servers" (*ebdomadarum ordinem*): cf. RB 35.

3.23 "who looks after the provisions of the brothers" (*qui cellarium fratrum contineat*): cf. RB 31. Like the major superior in the RIVP, this person is described here by his function, without a technical name or title.

3.25 "judgment" (*sententiam*): cf. Matt 26:24.

3.27 Cf. RB 31.8.

3.28 RB 31.8-10.

3.29 RB 32.4-5.

3.30 Cf. Dan 5:1-30.

3.31 Cf. RB 66.8.

[Chapter 11]

[15] How the weakness or strength of bodies should be recognized by him who presides. [16] If one of the brothers through fastings or work of the hands—[17] which the Apostle prescribes, *While working with our hands, let us not burden any of you* (1 Cor 4:12 + 1 Thess 2:9 = 2 Thess 3:8)—[18] is of such a sort that he has been overcome by weakness, the one who presides ought to see to it how that weakness should be borne. [19] But if such a brother is weak in spirit, he ought to be more frequently busied, considering the Apostle, how *he might restore his body to subjection* (1 Cor 9:27). [20] Moreover, this ought to be observed, that in nothing may he do his own will.

[Chapter 12]

[21] How the brothers ought to come before one another in mutual duties. [22] If the community of brothers is large, he who presides ought to determine the order of the weekly servers and duties which they should follow in ministering, each in turn.

[23] What sort of person he should be who looks after the provisions of the brothers. [24] Such a person ought to be chosen who can maintain control at all suggestions of gluttony, [25] who fears the judgment on Judas, who *from the beginning was a thief* (John 12:6 + 8:44). [26] He ought to be diligent who is delegated to this office, that he hear, [27] *He who has ministered well acquires a good position for himself* (1 Tim 3:13).

[28] The brothers ought to know, moreover, that whatever is used in the monastery, whether in [the form of] vessels or tools or all other things, is consecrated. [29] If anyone has used something negligently, [30] he should realize that he has a part with that king who drank with his mistresses from the consecrated vessels of the house of God and deserves such a punishment.

[31] These precepts ought to be observed and recounted daily into the ears of the brothers.

[XIII] Macharius dixit [1] quoniam veritas protestatur quae dicit: *In ore duorum vel trium testium stabit omne verbum;* [2] firma ergo est regula pietatis. [3] Nec tacendum est qualiter inter se monasteria pacem firmam obtineant. [4] Non licebit de alio monasterio sine voluntate eius qui praeest fratrem recipere— [5] non solum recipere sed nec videre oportet—, [6] dicente Apostolo quia *qui primam fidem inritam fecit est infideli deterior.* [7] Quod si praecatus fuerit eum qui sibi praeest ut in alio monasterio ingrediatur, commendetur ab eo ei qui praeest ubi esse desiderat, [8] et sic suscipiatur, [9] ut quantos fratres in monasterio invenerit, tantos se noverit habere priores. [10] Nec attendendum est quod fuit, sed probandum est qualis esse coeperit. [11] Susceptus vero si habere videtur aliquid sive in rebus sive in codicibus, ultra eum possidere non licebit, [12] ut possit *esse perfectus* qui alibi non potuit. [13] Residentibus vero fratribus, si fuerit aliqua de Scripturis conlatio et fuerit ex his talis scitus, non ei liceat loqui, nisi praeceptum fuerit ab eo qui praeest.

[XIV] [14] Qualiter clerici hospites suscipiantur. [15] Cum omni reverentia ut ministri altaris. [16] Non licebit nisi ipsi orationem complere; sive ostiarius sit, minister est templi Dei. [17] Quod si aliquo casu lapsus est et in eo quod dicitur probatus crimine, non eum liceat ante eum qui praeest vel secundum complere. [18] Nullo permittatur clerico in monasterio habitare, [19] nisi eis tantum quos lapsus peccati ad humilitatem deduxit et est vulneratus, ut in monasterio humilitatis medicina sanetur.

4.1 Matt 18:16 is also alluded to in RB 23.2; 58.6.

4.2 "guide to piety" (*regula pietatis*): see note on RIVP 1.17.

4.4 "him who presides" (*eius qui praeest*): this apparently refers to the superior of the monastery he wishes to leave, though the text is unclear; cf. RB 61.13-14.

4.9 Cf. RB 61.11-12.

4.11 Cf. RB 33.3.

4.16 "porter" (*ostiarius*): this is one of the minor orders.

4.18 RB 60 takes a different approach to the matter.

4.19 Cf. Ps 88(89):11.

4. Admission of Monastic Brothers from Other Houses Reception of Clerical Guests

[Chapter 13]

Macarius said [1] that the truth is borne out which says, *In the mouth of two or three witnesses every work will stand* (Matt 18:16 = 2 Cor 13:1 = Deut 19:15); [2] therefore, this guide to piety is firm. [3] And it should not be passed over in silence how monasteries should maintain a lasting peace among themselves. [4] It will not be permitted to receive a brother from another monastery without the approval of him who presides—[5] not only may one not receive him but not even see him—[6] in accord with the Apostle, who says that *he who makes his first faith void is worse than an unbeliever* (1 Tim 5:12, 8). [7] But if he should plead with him who is presiding to enter into another monastery, let him be commended by that superior to him who presides where he desires to be. [8] And let him be so received [9] that he should know that he has as many brothers above him as he finds in the monastery. [10] Nor should attention be paid to what he was; rather, what sort of person he has begun to be should be examined. [11] If, indeed, the one received is seen to possess something, whether in material goods or in codices, he will not be permitted to keep it any longer [12] so that he who was not able elsewhere can *be perfect* (Matt 5:48). [13] And if, when the brothers are assembled, there is a conference on the Scriptures and even though he is the learned one among them, it is not permitted for him to speak unless he is commanded by him who presides.

[Chapter 14]

[14] How clerical guests ought to be received—[15] with all reverence as ministers of the altar. [16] It will not be permitted [for anyone] except them to complete the prayer, even if one of them be a porter, because he is a minister of the temple of God. [17] But if he has lapsed in some case and is proven guilty of the crime that is spoken of, he may not be permitted to finish before him who presides or before the second in rank. [18] Let it not be permitted for any cleric to live in the monastery, [19] except him alone whom the lapse into sin has led to humility and he has been wounded, so that he may be healed by the medicine of humility in the monastery.

[20] Haec vobis tenenda sufficiant, custodienda conveniant, et *eritis inrepraehensibiles.*

[XV] [1] Nec hoc tacendum est, qualiter culpae singulorum emendentur. Pro qualitate culpae erit excommunicatio. Ergo iste ordo teneatur. [2] Si quis ex fratribus sermonem otiosum emiserit, [3] ne *reus sit concilii,* praecipimus eum triduo a fratrum congregatione vel colloquio alienum esse, ut nullus cum eo iungatur. [4] Si vero aliquis depraehensus fuerit in risu vel *scurrilitate* sermonis—[5] sicut dicit Apostolus: *Quae ad rem non pertinet*—, [6] iubemus huiusmodi duarum ebdomadarum *in nomine Domini* omni flagello humilitatis coherceri, [7] dicente Apostolo: *Si quis frater nominatur inter vos iracundus aut superbus aut maledicus,* [8] *hunc notate et nolite ut inimicum existimare, sed corripite ut fratrem;* [9] et alio loco: *Si quis frater fuerit praeventus in aliquo delicto, vos qui spiritales estis, instruite huiusmodi et corripite fratrem.* [10] Sic debet unusquisque vestrum instruere alium, ut per humilitatis frequentiam *non reprobus* sed probatus in congregatione perseveret.

[XVI] [11] Hoc ante omnia praecipimus vobis qui huic officio praesto estis ut *personae a vobis non accipiantur,* [12] sed aequali affectu omnes diligantur et correptione omnes sanentur, [13] quia aequalitas placet apud Deum, [14] dicente Propheta: *Si vere utique iustitiam loquimini, iusta iudicate.* [15] Hoc vobis latere nolumus quia qui non corripit errantem, noverit se pro eo *rationem redditurum.* [16] *Estote fideles* et boni cultores. [17] *Corripite inquietos, suscipite infirmos, patientes estote ad omnes,* [18] et quantos *fueritis lucrati, pro tantis mercedem accipietis;* [19] *in nomine Patris et Filii et Spiritus Sancti. Amen.*

5.0 Neufville suggests ("Règle," p. 50), on the basis of the language and tone, that this concluding section was added by another author but before 2RP, since these themes are also taken up by 2RP.

5.1 RB 24.1.

5.3 This scriptural passage is alluded to in RB 4.22. See RB 26.1 for content similar to this section.

5.4 Cf. RB 6.8.

5.10 This scriptural passage is quoted by RB 2.13; 4.11.

5.11 Cf. RB 2.16-20; 34.2.

5.12 "be loved" (*diligantur*): this is as close as the RIVP comes to stating the monastic virtue of love (*caritas*).

"with equal affection" (*aequali affectu*): cf. RB 2.22.

5.15 This scriptural passage is alluded to in RB 2.38.

5.18 This scriptural passage is alluded to in RB 23.2; 58.6.

²⁰ Let these things suffice for what ought to be followed by you, fitting for what needs to be kept, and *you will be blameless* (1 Tim 5:7).

5. Appendix: Correction

[Chapter 15]

¹ And it should not be passed over in silence, how faults of individuals ought to be amended. There will be an excommunication according to the gravity of the fault. Therefore, this procedure should be observed: ² If one of the brothers engages in idle talk, ³ in order that he may not *be answerable to the council* (Matt 5:22), we prescribe that for three days he be kept from the company of the brothers and from speaking so that no one may associate with him. ⁴ And if someone is caught laughing or using *scurrilous* language, *which does not,* ⁵ as the Apostle says, *pertain to the matter* (Eph 5:4), ⁶ we order that he be chastised *in the name of the Lord* (1 Cor 5:4) by every scourge of humility for two weeks, ⁷ in accord with the Apostle, who says, *If a brother is named among you as being irritable or proud or abusive* (1 Cor 5:11), ⁸ *take note of him and do not consider him as a brother* (2 Thess 3:14-15); ⁹ and in another passage, *If a brother is overtaken in any offense, you who are spiritual men, instruct him accordingly and correct the brother* (Gal 6:1). ¹⁰ Thus, each one of you ought to instruct another so that *not as one untested* (1 Cor 9:27) but tried by frequency of humility, he might persevere in the community.

[Chapter 16]

¹¹ This above all things we command you who are in this presiding office, that *there be no favoritism of persons* (Rom 2:11 + Eph 6:9 [cf. Jas 2:1]) on your part; ¹² rather, that all be loved with equal affection and all be cured through correction, ¹³ because equality is pleasing to God. ¹⁴ As the Prophet says, *If you indeed speak justice, make just judgments* (Ps 57[58]:2 [cf. Jas 2:4]).

¹⁵ We do not wish you to be ignorant of this, since he who does not correct the wayward shall know that *the reckoning will be accounted* (Heb 13:17) to him. ¹⁶ *Be faithful* (Rev 2:10) and good caretakers. ¹⁷ *Reprove the restless, give support to the weak, be patient to all* (1 Thess 5:14); ¹⁸ and as many as *you have gained,* for just as many *will you receive recompense* (Matt 18:15); ¹⁹ *in the name of the Father and of the Son and of the Holy Spirit. Amen* (Matt 28:19).

INCIPIT ALTERA REGULA PATRUM

[Praef.] [1] Residentibus nobis in unum *in nomine Domini Ihesu Christi* secundum traditionem patrum virorum sanctorum, [2] visum est nobis conscribere vel ordinare regulam quae in monasterio teneatur ad profectum fratrum, [3] ut neque nos laboremus, neque sanctus praepositus qui constitutus est in loco dubitationem aliquam patiatur, [4] ut omnes *unianimes*, sicut scriptum est, *et unum sentientes, invicem honorantes*, ea quae statuta sunt a Domino iugi observatione custodiant.

[I] [5] Ante omnia habentes *caritatem, humilitatem, patientiam, mansuetudinem* vel cetera quae docet sanctus Apostolus, [6] ita ut nemo suum quidquam vindicet, sed sicut scriptum est in Actus Apostolorum: *Habebant omnia communia.*
[7] Hunc autem qui praepositus est Dei iudicio et ordinatione sacerdotali in omnibus timere, diligere et obaudire secundum veritatem, [8] quia si quis se putat illum spernere Deum spernet, [9] sicut scriptum est: *Qui vos audit me audit, qui vos spernet me spernet et qui me spernet spernet eum qui me misit;* [10] ita ut sine ipsius voluntate nullus fratrum quidquam agat neque accipiat aliquid neque det nec usquam prorsus recedat sine verbo praecepti.

---

0 All references are made here to Neufville's versified text of 2RP. The chapter divisions [in brackets] correspond to those in the Migne text of Benedict of Aniane's *Codex regularum* (PL 103, cols. 441–444).

1 This rule begins similarly to RIVP Pr 1.

2 "rule" (*regulam*): here the term has the technical sense of monastic rule; see notes on RIVP Pr 3; 1.7.

3 "holy superior" (*sanctus praepositus*): this is the usual term in 2RP for the head of the monastery, much like "abbot" (*abbas*) in later rules.

4 Rom 12:10 is quoted by RB 63.17; 72.4 and alluded to in RB 72.7.

5 Cf. also 2RP 21, where another scriptural quotation concerning love is cited; this is an indication of the rule's concern for the interior life of the monastic brothers; see Neufville, "Règle," p. 50.

7 This does not mean that the superior is a priest but that he is blessed by the bishop, as in RM 93.56, 59, 62; see A. de Vogüé, *Community and Abbot in the Rule of Saint Benedict*, vol. 1, trans. Charles Philippi, in Cistercian Studies Series, no. 5

THE SECOND RULE OF THE FATHERS

[Preface]

¹ As we were sitting together *in the name of our Lord Jesus Christ* (1 Cor 5:4), according to the custom of the Fathers, holy men, ² it seemed good to us to put together in writing and set in order a rule that might be kept in the monastery for the progress of the brothers; ³ so that we might neither be troubled nor might the holy superior who has been placed in that office suffer any doubt: ⁴ so that *all of one mind*, as it is written, and *of one heart, honoring each other* (Phil 2:2 + Rom 12:10), might keep with constant observance those precepts that have been established by the Lord.

[Chapter 1]

⁵ Preferring above all things *love, humility, patience, gentleness* (1 Tim 6:11 + Eph 4:2) and those other things that the holy Apostle teaches, ⁶ no one will claim anything as his own, but, as it is written in the Acts of the Apostles, *they held all things in common* (Acts 2:44). ⁷ Fear, love, and obey in all things according to truth the one who is superior by the judgment of God and priestly ordination. ⁸ And if someone believes that he despises him, he is actually despising God; ⁹ as it is written, *He who listens to you, listens to me; he who despises you, despises me; and he who despises me, despises the one who sent me* (Luke 10:16). ¹⁰ So, let no brother do anything without his approval, nor accept anything, nor give anything, nor go anywhere without his express command.

(Kalamazoo, Mich.: Cistercian Publications, 1979) 7, and his "Introduction" to *The Rule of the Master*, trans. Luke Eberle, in Cistercian Studies Series, no. 6 (Kalamazoo, Mich.: Cistercian Publications, 1977) 58–59.

9 This scriptural passage is quoted by RB 5.6, 15.

10 "no brother" (*nullus fratrum*): as in RIVP, "brothers" is the designation for monastic members. The word "monk" (*monachus*) is not used in this rule. Cf. RB 33.2; 49.10.

[II] [11] Observari etiam hoc debet ut non se invicem fabulis vanis destruant, sed unusquisque operam suam et meditem suum custodiat et *cogitatum habeat ad Dominum*. [12] In conventu omnium nullus iuniorum quidquam loquatur nisi interrogatus. [13] Ceterum si quis vult consolationis accipere vel verbi audire secretum, opportunum tempus requirat.

[III] [14] Advenienti peregrino nihil plus exibeat quam occursum humilem et pacem. [15] Reliquum non sit illi cura unde venerit vel quid venerit vel quando ambulaturus sit, [16] nec se iungat ad fabulas cum illo.

[IV] [17] Illud quoque observandum est ut praesente seniore quocumque vel praecedente in ordine psallendi, sequens non habeat facultatem loquendi vel aliquid praesumendi, [18] nisi tantum is qui in ordine, ut dictum est, praecedere videtur, [19] hoc usque ad imum, ante omnia in oratione sive in opere sive in responso dando. [20] Si vero simplicior fuerit vel imperitior sermone et dederit locum, ita demum sequens loquatur. [21] *Omnia tamen in caritate fiant*, non *per contentionem vel aliquam praesumptionem*.

[V] [22] Cursus vero vel orationum vel psalmorum, sicut dudum statutum est, vel tempus meditandi operandique servabitur. [23] Ita meditem habeant fratres ut usque ad horam tertiam legant, [24] si tamen nulla causa extiterit qua necesse sit etiam praetermisso medite aliquid fieri in commune. [25] Post horam vero tertiam unusquisque *ad opus* suum *paratus sit* usque ad horam nonam [26] vel quidquid iniunctum fuerit *sine murmuratione*

---

11 "meditation" (*meditem*): this Latin word is not attested elsewhere; perhaps it is the Latinization of a Greek word. It has the sense here of the "rumination of Scripture," i.e., the memorization of it; cf. also 5.23-24. In Clément's *Lexique*, p. 710, it is equated with *meditationem*.

14-16 This is a distillation of the injunctions governing the reception of guests already set forth in RIVP 2.36-42.

14 "let one offer" (*exibeat*): it is unclear whether this person is the superior or any of the monastic brothers. RIVP 2.37-40 suggests that only the superior or those to whom he delegates this duty can receive and have anything to do with the guests.

"peace" (*pacem*): this refers to the kiss of peace.

17-21 This section parallels that of RIVP 2.10-15.

23-26 This injunction accords with that in RIVP 3.10-12, but by the time of RMac and 3RP the third hour has been changed to the second.

[Chapter 2]

[11] This must also be observed, that they do not harm each other with useless talk, but let everyone watch over his own work and meditation and *keep his thoughts towards the Lord* (Ps 54[55]:23). [12] In the assembly of all, let no junior say anything unless asked. [13] As for the rest, if someone wants to receive comfort or hear a word in private, let him seek an opportune time.

[Chapter 3]

[14] Let one offer to an arriving traveler nothing more than a humble reception and peace; [15] let him not be otherwise concerned—where he came from, why he came, or when he is going to leave; [16] nor let him participate in useless talk with him.

[Chapter 4]

[17] This also must be observed, that whenever any senior or anyone who precedes him in the order of singing the psalms is present, the one who follows may not be allowed to speak or to take an initiative, [18] but only the one who precedes, as has been said. [19] This shall be observed down to the last in order, especially in prayer, whether in work or in giving response. [20] If, however, the one who precedes should be of a more simple mind or less skilled in speech and gives up his place, only then may the one who follows in order speak. [21] But *let all things be done in love* (1 Cor 16:14; Phil 2:3), not through contentiousness or any presumption.

[Chapter 5]

[22] The course of prayers and psalms and the time for meditation and work shall be observed just as it has already been established. [23] Let the brethren have meditation so that they may read until the third hour, [24] provided that there be no necessity for something to be done in common, at which time the meditation is then omitted. [25] Then after the third hour, let each one *be ready at his task* (2 Tim 2:21) until the ninth hour, [26] and let him complete whatever has been enjoined upon him *without*

vel haesitatione perficiant sicut docet sanctus Apostolus. [27] Si quis autem murmuraverit vel contentiosus exteterit aut opponens in aliquo contraria voluntate praeceptis, [28] digne correptus secundum arbitrium praepositi tamdiu abstineatur quamdiu vel culpae qualitas poposcerit vel se paenitendo humiliaverit atque emendaverit. [29] Correptus autem non audeat usquam recedere. [30] Si quis vero de fratribus vel qui in monasterio sunt vel qui per cellulis consistunt eius errori consenserit, excommunicatione dignissimus habeatur.

[VI] [31] Ad horam vero orationis dato signo, si quis non statim praetermisso omni opere quod agit—quia nihil orationi praeponendum est—paratus fuerit, foris excludatur confundendus. [32] Operam vero dabunt singulis fratribus ut tempore quo missae fiunt sive per diem sive per noctem, quando diutius ad oratione standum est, non deficiant vel superfluo foris secedant, [33] quia scriptum est in evangelio: *Oportet semper orare et non deficere*, [34] et alio loco: *Non impediaris orare semper*. [35] Si quis autem non necessitate sed magis vitio secedere putaverit, sciat se cum depraehensus fuerit culpabilem iudicandum, [36] quia per suam neglegentiam et alios in vitio mittit. [37] In vigiliis vero observandum est quando omnes conveniunt, quicumque gravatur somno et exit foras non se fabulis occupet, [38] sed statim redeat ad opus quod convenitur. [39] In congregatione autem ipsa ubi legitur, aurem semper ad Scripturas habeant et silentium observent omnes.

---

27 Cf. Matt 20:11; 1 Cor 11:16. This last scriptural passage is also alluded to in RB 71.5.

28 "and" (*vel . . . vel*): in the Latin of this time, *vel* often has the weakened sense of "and" instead of "or."

29 "to retreat anywhere" (*usquam recedere*): the context suggests that the reprimanded brother might seek refuge and comfort from the semi-anchorites living near the cenobium.

30 Cf. 2 Thess 2:12.

"monastery . . . cells" (*monasterio . . . cellulis*): the monastery here refers to the cenobium, which was surrounded by the dwellings of "cells" of semi-anchorites; cf. RMac 13.1.

31-46 RMac 14-18 borrows from this entire last section of 2RP.

31 Cf. RB 43.1-3; this passage seems to be the immediate source for Benedict's dictum, "Nothing is to be preferred to the Work of God."

32 "office" (*missae*): this has the meaning of liturgical prayer; see also RMac 15.2; RO 32.8.

murmuring or hesitation (Phil 2:14), as the holy Apostle teaches.
[27] If, however, someone should murmur, be contentious, or re-
sist anything with a will contrary to commands, [28] after he has
been suitably reproved according to the judgment of the superior, let him be excluded as long as the nature of the fault demands it and until he humbles himself by doing penance and
makes amends. [29] After he has been reproached, let him not
dare to retreat anywhere. [30] If any of the brothers, either of
those who are in the monastery or those who are in the cells,
concurs in his error, he shall be most deserving of excom-
munication.

[Chapter 6]

[31] At the hour of prayer, when the signal has been given, he
who has not immediately set aside any task that he is doing and
is not ready (since nothing ought to come before prayer) should
be shut outside so that he may be shamed. [32] They will see to it
that all of the brothers not falter nor go out of doors unnecessari-
ly at the time of office, whether during the day or at night, when
it is necessary to remain longer at prayer; [33] because it is written
in the Gospel, *It is necessary indeed to pray always, and not to cease*
(Luke 18:1). [34] And in another passage, *You shall not be hindered
from praying always* (Sir 18:22). [35] If someone, however, should
decide to go out, not because of necessity but rather because of
vice, let him know that when he has been found out, he shall be
judged culpable, [36] because through his negligence he also leads
others into vice. [37] During the vigils, this must be observed:
when all gather together, let whoever is heavy with sleep and
goes outside not occupy himself with talk, [38] but let him return
immediately to the work for which all are gathered together.
[39] Moreover, in the gathering itself when there is reading, let
them always keep their ears attentive to the Scriptures, and let
all observe silence.

---

33 This scriptural passage is alluded to in RB 4.56.
35-36 Cf. RB 43.8.

[VII] [40] Hoc etiam addendum fuit ut frater qui pro qualibet culpa arguitur vel increpatur patientiam habeat et non respondeat arguenti, sed humiliet se in omnibus, [41] secundum
praeceptum Domini dicentis quia *Deus superbis resistit, humilibus
autem dat gratiam,* [42] et *qui se humiliat exaltabitur.* [43] Qui vero
saepius correptus non se emendaverit, novissimus in ordine
stare iubeatur. [44] Qui nec sic quidem emendaverit, extraneus
habeatur, [45] sicut Dominus dixit: *Sit tibi sicut ethnicus et publicanus.*

[46] Ad mensa autem specialiter nullus loquatur nisi qui praeest
vel qui interrogatus fuerit.

40-46 Cf. RIVP 5.1-10 on correction.
40 Cf. 2 Tim 4:2. This scriptural passage is quoted by RB 2.23 and alluded to in
RB 58.11.
42 This scriptural passage is quoted by RB 7.1.
45 This scriptural passage is alluded to in RB 23.3.

[Chapter 7]

[40] This also must be added, that a brother who for whatever fault is reproved or chastised have patience, and let him not talk back to the person who is reproving him; rather, let him humble himself in all things, [41] according to the precept of the Lord, who says, *For God gives grace to the humble but resists the proud* (Jas 4:6 = 1 Pet 5:5 [cf. Prov 3:34 LXX]). And, [42] *whoever humbles himself shall be exalted* (Luke 14:11). [43] Truly, let him who is reprimanded more often and has not corrected himself be commanded to stand last in rank. [44] And let him who has not corrected himself even then be held a stranger, [45] as the Lord says, *Let him be to you as a heathen and tax collector* (Matt 18:17). [46] But let no one speak, especially at table, except the one who presides or whoever has been asked.

INCIPIT REGULA MACHARII ABBATIS

I. [1] Milites ergo Christi sic taliter suos debent componere gressus [2] caritatem inter se perfectissimam continentes [3] Deum ex tota anima diligere et ex tota mente et ex toto corde et ex tota virtute sua.

II. [1] Invicem inter se perfectissimam sectantes oboedientiam, [2] pacifici, mites, moderati, [3] non superbi, non iniuriosi, non susurrones, non inrisores, non verbosi, non praesumptiosi, [4] non sibi placentes sed ei, cui militant, Christo, [5] non blasfemiam sectantes nec dedicere quemquam, [6] ad obsequium non pigri, ad orationem parati, in humilitate perfecti, [7] in oboedientia praecincti, in vigiliis instantes, in ieiunio hilares.

III. [1] Nullus se ab alio iustiorem arbitretur, [2] sed unusquisque ab omnibus se inferiorem contemnat, [3] quia *qui se exaltat humiliabitur et qui se humiliat exaltabitur.*

IV. [1] Praeceptum senioris ut salutem suscipias. [2] Non murmurando ullam operam facias. [3] Non responsionem contra praeceptum usurpes.

V. [1] Non te extollas aut magnifices aliquam utilem fecisse operam. [2] Non in adquirendo aliquid lucri congaudeas [3] nec in damno contristes.

1.0 The versification of this rule follows the text of Helga Styblo.
2.1 Cf. RB 71.1.
2.2-3 Cf. RO 30.1.

THE RULE OF MACARIUS

Chapter 1

[1-2] The soldiers of Christ, possessing among themselves most perfect charity, must so order their steps [3] *to love God with one's whole soul, with one's whole mind, with one's whole heart, and with one's whole strength* (Mark 12:30).

Chapter 2

[1] Mutually striving after most perfect obedience, [2] let them be peace-loving, gentle, moderate, [3] not proud, not abusive, not murmurers, not scoffers, not talkative, not presumptuous, [4] not self-indulgent, but pleasing to God, whose Christ they serve. [5] Neither pursuing blasphemy nor contradicting anyone, [6] let them not be slow in compliance, [but] ready for prayer, perfect in humility, [7] girded in obedience, alert during vigils, happy while fasting.

Chapter 3

[1] Let no one consider himself more just than another, [2] but let each one disparage himself as inferior to all, [3] for *he who exalts himself shall be humbled, and he who humbles himself shall be exalted* (Luke 14:11 [cf. Matt 23:12]).

Chapter 4

[1] Accept the precept of an elder as a blessing; [2] do not perform any task grudgingly; [3] make no complaint against a precept.

Chapter 5

[1] Do not extol yourself or glory in having done some useful task; [2] do not rejoice in acquiring any gain [3] or sorrow in any loss.

VI. [1] Nec te familiaritas ulla ad saeculum trahat, [2] sed tota dilectio vestra in cellula demoretur. [3] Cellam ut paradisum habeas, [4] fratres tuos spiritales ut aeternos confidas parentes.

VII. [1] Praepositum monasterii timeas ut Deum, diligas ut parentem. [2] Similiter quoque et omnes oportet diligere fratres, [3] cum quibus etiam te confidis videre in gloriam Christi.

VIII. [1] Non oderis laboriosam operam. [2] Otium quoque ne secteris. [3] In vigiliis confectus, in opere iusto madefactus ambulesque dormitans, [4] lassus ad stratum venias, cum Christo requiescere te credas.

IX. [1] Cursumque monasterii super omnia diligas. [2] Qui vero saepius orare voluerit, [3] uberiorem inveniet misericordiam Christi.

X. [1] Matutinumque dictum ita meditationem habeant fratres usque ad horam secundam, [2] si tamen nulla causa extiterit, [3] qua necesse sit etiam praetermissa meditatione aliquid fieri in commune.

XI. [1] Post horam vero secundam unusquisque ad opus suum paratus sit usque ad horam nonam [2] vel quid iniunctum fuerit, sine murmuratione perficiat, [3] sicut docet sanctus Apostolus.

XII. [1] Si quis autem murmuraverit vel contentiosus extiterit [2] aut resedens in aliquo contrariam voluntatem praeceptis,

---

7.1 "superior" (*praepositum*): here the term refers to the major superior of the monastery, whereas in 27.4 a distinction is made between the prior (*praepositus*), who is second in command, and the abbot (*abbati*) who is first in command.

9.0 Chs. 9–18 closely follow the concluding part of 2RP, on which they are based: chs. 9–13 (= 2RP 22-30) speak of prayer and work in the monastery; chs. 14–15 (= 2RP 31-39) discuss those who are late for the Work of God; chs. 16–18 (= 2RP 40-46) deal with correction.

10.1 In 2RP 23, the meditation lasts until the third hour; cf. RB 48.10ff., where even more detailed instructions are given.

10.2-3 Cf. RO 24.1-2.

11.1 RB 48.11 has the same injunction.

12.0 Cf. RO 32; RB 23.

Chapter 6

[1] Let no worldly friendship allure you, [2] but let all your happiness reside in your cell. [3] Regard your cell as paradise; [4] trust in your spiritual brothers as your eternal family.

Chapter 7

[1] Fear the superior of the monastery as God, love him as a parent. [2] Similarly, it is also necessary to love all the brothers, [3] with whom you expect to find yourself in the glory of Christ.

Chapter 8

[1] *Hate not arduous work* (Sir 7:16); [2] also do not be a follower of idleness. [3] Exhausted by vigils, worn out by just toil, walking as though asleep, [4] go to your bed weary and believe that you rest with Christ.

Chapter 9

[1] Love the observance of the monastery above all things. [2] For he who wishes to pray more often [3] shall find Christ's mercy more copious.

Chapter 10

[1] After matins have been said, let the brothers then have meditation until the second hour, [2] provided that there be no necessity [3] for something to be done in common, at which time the meditation is then omitted.

Chapter 11

[1] Then after the second hour, let each one be ready at his task until the ninth hour, [2] and let him complete *without murmuring* (Phil 2:14), whatever has been enjoined upon him, [3] as the holy Apostle teaches.

Chapter 12

[1] If, however, someone should murmur, be contentious, [2] or maintain his will with regard to something contrary to com-

[3] digne correptus secundum arbitrium senioris vel modum culpae [4] tamdiu abstineatur quamdiu culpae qualitas poposcerit [5] vel se paenitendo humiliaverit vel emendaverit ita, [6] ut correptus frater non audeat usquam recidere.

XIII. [1] Si qui vero de fratribus, vel qui in oratorio sunt vel qui per cellulas consistunt, [2] eius errori consenserit culpabilis erit.

XIV. [1] Ad horam vero orationis dato signo [2] qui non statim praetermisso omni opere quod agit occurrerit, [3] quia nihil orationi praeponendum est, [4] foris excludatur ut erubescat.

XV. [1] Operam vero dabunt singuli fratres [2] ut tempore quo missae fiunt in vigiliis observandum est, [3] quando omnes conveniunt. [4] Quicumque gravatur somno, [5] exeat foris, non se fabulis occupet, [6] sed statim redeat ad opus, quod convenitur. [7] In congregatione autem ipsa, ubi legitur, [8] aurem semper ad Scripturas habeat et silentium observent omnes.

XVI. [1] Hoc etiam addendum fuit, [2] ut frater qui pro qualibet culpa arguitur vel increpatur, [3] patientiam habeat et non respondeat arguenti se, [4] sed humiliet se in omnibus secundum praeceptum Domini dicentis [5] quia *Deus humilibus dat gratiam superbis autem resistit* [6] et *qui se humiliat exaltabitur.*

12.3 "the elder's" (*senioris*): this is the only occurrence of the term in this rule and probably refers to the abbot; cf. 2RP 28.

13.0 Cf. RO 33.

13.1 "oratory . . . cells" (*oratorio . . . cellulas*): here "oratory" is another word for "cenobium"; cf. 2RP 30.

14.2 Cf. RB 43.1.

14.3 Cf. RB 43.3.

16.2-4 Cf. RO 34.

mands, [3] after he has been suitably reproved according to the elder's judgment and the measure of the fault, [4] let him be excluded as long as the nature of the fault demands it, [5] and until he humbles himself by doing penance and makes amends [6] so that a brother who has been so reproached dare not lapse in any way.

Chapter 13

[1] If one of the brothers, either of those who are in the oratory or those who are in the cells, [2] concurs in his error, he shall be culpable.

Chapter 14

[1] At the hour of prayer, when the signal has been given, [2] he who has not immediately set aside any task that he is doing and does not hasten, [3] since nothing ought to come before prayer, [4] should be shut outside so that he may be shamed.

Chapter 15

[1] The individual brothers will give heed [2] to what must be observed during the office of vigils, [3] when all are gathered together. [4] Let whoever is heavy with sleep [5] go outside; let him not occupy himself with stories, [6] but let him return immediately to the work, which is going on. [7] Moreover, in the gathering itself where there is reading, [8] let him always keep his ears attentive to the Scriptures; let all of them observe silence.

Chapter 16

[1] This also must be given attention— [2] that a brother who for whatever fault is reproved or chastised [3] have patience, and let him not talk back to the person who is reproving him; [4] rather, let him humble himself in all things, according to the precept of the Lord, who says, [5] *For God gives grace to the humble but resists the proud* (Jas 4:6 [cf. 1 Pet. 5:5]) and [6] *whoever humbles himself shall be exalted* (Luke 14:11).

XVII. [1] Qui vero saepius correptus non se emendat [2] novissimus in ordine stare iubeatur. [3] Qui se nec sic quidem emendaverit [4] extraneus habeatur, sicut Dominus dixit: *Sit tibi sicut ethnicus et publicanus.*

XVIII. [1] Ad mensam autem specialiter nullus loquatur, [2] nisi qui praeest vel qui interrogatus fuerit.

XIX. [1] Nullus se in sua peritia neque in voce exaltet, [2] sed per humilitatem et oboedientiam laetetur in Domino.

XX. [1] *Hospitalitatem sectantes* per omnia et ne avertas oculos inanem relinquens pauperem, [2] ne forte Dominus in hospite aut in paupere ad te veniat [3] et videat te haesitantem et condemneris, [4] sed omnibus te hilarem ostende et fideliter age.

XXI. [1] Passus iniuriam taceas. [2] Iniuriam facere non nosse, factam posse tolerare. [3] Non te inania seducant consilia, [4] sed magis te semper in Christo confirma. [5] Non tibi ullos aestimes proximiores parentes quam [6] qui tecum sunt tui in cellula fratres.

XXII. [1] Si ad necessaria quaerenda in cellula bini egrediantur vel terni fratres [2] et ita illi, quibus credendum est, [3] non qui verbositatem aut gulam sectantur.

17.0 Cf. RO 32; 35.
18.0 Cf. RO 36; RB 38.5ff.
19.0 This chapter has no clear parallel in the Rules of the Fathers.
20.1-2 Cf. RB 53.15. Note the different emphasis in RO 40.1.
21.1-2 Cf. RB 4.30.
22.1-2 Cf. RO 22.1-3.
22.1 "cell" (*cellula*): this is another term for "monastery."

Chapter 17

[1] Truly, let him who is reprimanded more often and has not corrected himself [2] be commanded to stand last in rank. [3] Let him who has not corrected himself even thus [4] be considered a stranger; as the Lord says, *Let him be to you as a heathen and tax collector* (Matt 18:17).

Chapter 18

[1] But let no one speak, especially at table, [2] except the one who presides or whoever has been asked.

Chapter 19

[1] Let no one pride himself in his skill or in his voice, [2] but let him *rejoice in the Lord* (Phil 4:4) through humility and obedience.

Chapter 20

[1] *Pursuing hospitality* (Rom 12:13) in all things, do not avert your eye and abandon a pauper empty-handed, [2] lest by chance the Lord come to you in a guest or in a pauper [3] and see you hesitating, and you be condemned; [4] but show yourself hospitable to all and act with faith.

Chapter 21

[1] Having suffered an injury, be silent about it. [2] Do not know [what it is] to do an injury; be able to tolerate an injury done [to you]. [3] Let not inane counsels seduce you; [4] rather, always strengthen yourself in Christ. [5] Do not consider any to be closer parents to you than [6] those who are brothers with you in the cell.

Chapter 22

[1] When necessities are sought for the cell, let the brothers go out by two's or three's; [2] let them be such who are trusted, [3] not who follow gossip or their appetite.

XXIII. [1] Ergo si de saeculo quis in monasterio converti voluerit, [2] regula ei introeunti legatur et omnis actus monasterii illi patefiat. [3] Quod si omnia apte susceperit, sic digne a fratribus in cellula suscipiatur.

XXIV. [1] Nam si aliquam in cellulam voluerit inferre substantiam, [2] in mensa ponatur coram omnibus fratribus velut regula continet. [3] Quod si susceptum fuerit, non solum de substantia, quam intulit, [4] sed etiam nec de se ipsum ab illa iudicabit hora. [5] Nam si aliquid prius erogavit pauperibus aut veniens in cellula aliquid intulit fratribus, [6] ipsi tamen non est licitum, ut aliquid in sua habeat potestate.

XXV. [1] Quod si ex qualibet causa scandali post tertium diem inde exire voluerit, [2] nihil penitus nisi vestem in qua venit accipiat. [3] Aut si casu transierit, nullus heredum eius adire debet. [4] Quod si impulsare voluerit, [5] regula ei legatur et confundatur turpiter et discedat confusus, [6] quia et illi a quo repetit fuerit recitata.

XXVI. [1] Ergo ex qualibet causa quis peccaverit frater, [2] ab oratione suspendatur et ieiuniis distringatur. [3] Quod si coram omnibus fratribus prostratus veniam petierit, dimittatur illi.

XXVII. [1] Nam si in sua voluerit perseverare nequitia et superbia et dicat: [2] Hoc ego durare non possum, sed accipiam casulam meam et eam, ubi mihi placuerit. [3] Quis de fratribus hoc

---

23.0 RO 27 also treats the reception of postulants; cf. RIVP 2.16-35.
23.2 Cf. RB 58.12.
24.1, 3-4 Cf. RIVP 4.11.
24.2 "on the table" (*in mensa*): the word *mensa* already by the time of Ambrose and Augustine could mean "altar" and may have that meaning here as well; cf. 2RP 46 and RMac 18.1, where *mensa* clearly means a dining table.
24.5-6 Cf. RB 58.24.
25.0 This chapter refers to postulants who leave. A more severe treatment is reserved for monks; cf. 28.1-3.
25.1 "contention" (*scandali*): see the note on this term in *RB 1980*, pp. 208–209.
26.1-2 Cf. RB 25.1.
26.3 Cf. RB 44.
27.0 Cf. RO 32.

Chapter 23

[1] Thus, if someone from the world should wish to be converted in the monastery, [2] let the rule be read to him when he enters, and let every practice of the monastery be made clear to him. [3] And if he should accept all things suitably, let him thus be fittingly received by the brothers in the cell.

Chapter 24

[1] Now if he should wish to bring some possession into the cell, [2] let it be put on the table in front of all the brothers, as the rule requires. [3-4] And, if it has been accepted, he shall not from that hour be the judge, not only of the property that he brought but even of himself. [5] For though he bestowed something on the poor beforehand, or, on coming into the cell, brought something for the brothers, [6] nevertheless it is not permitted for him to have anything in his possession.

Chapter 25

[1] If for some reason of contention he should wish to leave after the third day, [2] let him take nothing at all except the clothing in which he came. [3] Or in the case that he should by chance die, none of his heirs must come. [4] And if one of them should wish to exert pressure, [5] let the rule be read to him, and let him be shamefully confounded, and let him leave in confusion, [6] because also to him from whom he demands, it had been recited.

Chapter 26

[1] Thus let the brother who sins from whatever cause [2] be suspended from prayer and be strictured with fasts. [3] If he should ask forgiveness, prostrated in front of all the brothers, let him be forgiven.

Chapter 27

[1] For if he should wish to persevere in his wickedness and pride and say, [2] "I cannot bear this, but I shall take my little hut and go where I like," [3] let whoever of the brothers first heard

eum loquentem prius audierit, [4] referat praeposito et praepositus abbati. [5] Abbas coram omnibus resedeat fratribus, [6] eum exhiberi praecipiat, virgis emendato oratio fiat et sic ad communionem recipiatur. [7] Quia qui sana non emendantur doctrina, virgis purgantur.

XXVIII. [1] Quod si casu quis frater de cella de qualibet causa scandali exire voluerit, [2] nihil penitus nisi nugacissimo induatur vestitu [3] et extra communionem infidelis discedat. [4] Nam quieti et pacifici excelsum diripiunt regnum [5] et ut filii computabuntur altissimi aut pretiosas et splendidas accipiunt coronas. [6] Filii autem tenebrarum in exteriores ibunt tenebras. [7] Super quem requiescam, dicit Dominus, nisi super humilem et quietum et trementem verba mea?

XXIX. [1] Ita hoc observandum est, [2] quod quarta et sexta feria qui infrangunt ieiunium, gravem sibi poenam adquirunt.

XXX. [1] Illud etiam addendum fuit, [2] ut intra monasterium artificium non faciat ullus, [3] nisi ille, cuius fides probata fuerit, [4] qui ad utilitatem et necessitatem monasterii faciat, quid poterit facere.

27.6 Cf. RB 28.1.
27.7 Cf. RB 23.5.

him say this [4] refer it to the prior, and the prior to the abbot. [5] Let the abbot sit in front of all the brothers, [6] and let him order that he be shown forth; and after he has been purged with rods, let a prayer be said, and thus let him be received back into the community. [7] For those who are not corrected by sound doctrine should be purged with rods.

Chapter 28

[1] If perchance some brother should wish to leave the cell for some reason of contention, [2] let him wear nothing except the most ragged clothes, [3] and let him depart as a faithless one outside the community. [4] For *the calm and peaceful plunder the heavenly kingdom* [5] *and shall be counted as sons of the Most High* (Matt 5:9; 5:45; Luke 6:35) and shall receive precious and splendid crowns; [6] however, the sons of darkness shall go into outer darkness: [7] *Upon whom shall I rest, says the Lord, unless upon the humble man, both calm and trembling at my words?* (Is 66:2).

Chapter 29

[1] This must be observed, [2] that those who break the fast during the fourth and sixth weekday acquire for themselves a grievous punishment.

Chapter 30

[1] This also must be attended to— [2] that inside the monastery no one practice a craft [3] except him of proven faith, [4] who does what he is able to do for the utility and necessity of the monastery.

INCIPIT TERTIA PATRUM REGULA
AD MONACHOS

I. [1] Cum in nomine Domini, una cum fratribus nostris convenissemus, imprimis placuit ut regula et instituta patrum per ordinem legerentur: [2] quibus lectis placuit, [3] si de saeculo quis in monasterio converti voluerit, [4] regula ei introeunti legatur, et omnes actus monasterii illi patefiant. [5] Quod si omnia apte susceperit, sic digne a fratribus in cellula suscipiatur, [6] tum si aliquam in cellulam voluerit inferre substantiam, in mensa ponatur coram omnibus fratribus, velut regula continet. [7] Quod si susceptus fuerit, non solum de substantia quam intulit, sed etiam nec de seipso ab illa iudicabit hora.

II. [1] Abbati vero nulli liceat sibi quidquam proprie vindicare [2] cum omnia Deo propitio in illius maneant potestate. [3] Si quis vero, quod in regula iunioribus prohibetur, sibi aliquid ex successione parentum, seu quolibet donato retinere praesumpserit, et non omnia in commune posuerit, a fratribus arguatur. [4] Si in vitio perstiterit, in notitiam episcopi deferatur: [5] qui si ab episcopo correptus nec sic emendaverit, deponatur.

III. [1] Vestimenta vero fratribus necessaria ita abbas omnibus ordinare debet, quae monachis deceant; [2] non diversis coloribus tincta, exceptis cucullis quae comparantur, si fuerint nigrae, uti eas debere censemus.

1.0 For convenience in cross reference, the textual versification used by Desprez has been employed here.

1.1-5 RMac 23; cf. RB 58.12.

1.1 This opening formula is reminiscent of those at the beginning of episcopal synods; see Mundó, p. 119; cf. RIVP Pr 1; 2RP 1.

1.6-7 RMac 24.

2.1 "any abbot" (*abbati vero nulli*): the superior of the monastery is now called "abbot."

2.5 RB 64.4 requires episcopal intervention when a community has chosen an unworthy abbot.

THE THIRD RULE OF THE FATHERS

Chapter 1

[1] When we convened together with our brothers in the name of the Lord, it seemed good that at the very first the rule and institutes of the Fathers be read in order. [2] After these things were read, [3] it seemed appropriate that when someone wants to be converted from the world to the monastery, [4] the rule be read to him when he enters, and all the ways of the monastery be made clear to him. [5] And if he should uphold all things suitably, let him thus be fittingly received by the brothers. [6] Now if he should wish to bring some possession into the cell, let it be put on the table in front of all the brothers, as the rule requires. [7] Because if he has been received, he shall not from that hour be the judge, not only of the property that he brought but even of himself.

Chapter 2

[1] Let it not be allowed for any abbot to claim anything as his own, [2] although through God's favor all things remain in his power. [3] If some abbot should not place everything in common but should presume to keep for himself something that he has inherited from his family or something that has been given to him and that the rule forbids other monks to keep, let him be reprimanded by the brothers. [4] If he should persist in his sin, let him be brought to the attention of the bishop. [5] And if he should not amend after being chastised by the bishop, let him be deposed.

Chapter 3

The abbot must arrange for the clothes necessary for all the brothers, such as are suitable for monks. They should not be dyed in different colors, except for the cowls that are bought already black; we believe they must be used.

IV. [1] Familiaritatem omnium mulierum, tam parentum quam extranearum, pro custodienda vita vel cavendis laqueis diaboli, ab omnibus monasteriis vel culturis monachorum; seu frequentationem monachorum a monasteriis puellarum, sicut regula docet, prohibere censemus. [2] Neque ulla mulier in interius atrium monasterii ingredi audeat. [3] Quod si cum consilio vel voluntate abbatis monasterium vel cellulas monachorum quaedam fuerit ingressa, [4] merito ipse abbas et nomen abbatis deponat, et inferiorem se omnibus presbyteris recognoscat, [5] quia talis sancto gregi praeponi debet, qui eos immaculatos Deo offerre procuret; non per quaslibet familiaritates diabolo sociare festinet.

V. [1] Matutino dicto fratres lectioni vacent usque ad horam secundam: [2] si tamen nulla causa exstiterit qua necesse sit etiam praetermissa lectione aliquid fieri in commune. [3] Post horam secundam unusquisque ad opus suum paratus sit usque ad horam nonam: [4] quod iniunctum fuerit, sine murmuratione perficiat.

VI. [1] Ad horam vero orationis dato signo, [2] qui non statim praetermisso omni opere quod agit, quia nihil orationi praeponendum est, paratus fuerit, ab abbate vel praeposito corripiatur: [3] et nisi prostratus veniam petierit, excommunicetur.

VII. Ad mensam autem specialiter nullus loquatur, nisi qui praeest, vel qui interrogatus fuerit.

4.0 Mundó, p. 120, n. 35, points out that similar injunctions are found in the decrees of various Gallic councils, including that of Agde in 506, chs. X–XI and XXVIII (PL 84, cols. 265 and 267).

5.0 Closely parallels RMac 10–11.

6.0 While this parallels RMac 14, the punishment is different.

7.0 RMac 18.

Chapter 4

[1] For the sake of guarding one's life and fearing the devil's snares, we propose to prohibit, in accordance with the rule, the close acquaintance of women, whether relatives or strangers, from all monasteries or the lands of the monks, as well as to prohibit monks from frequenting the monasteries of virgins, as the rule teaches. [2] Nor shall any woman dare to come into the entrance-hall of the monastery. [3] And if some woman should enter the monastery or the cells of the monks with the consent or approval of the abbot, [4] he should deservedly both give up the name of abbot and recognize himself as inferior to all the presbyters, [5] because the man set over the holy flock must be one who takes care to offer them immaculate to God, not one who hastens to join them to the devil through familiarities of any sort.

Chapter 5

[1] After the matins have been said, let the monks be occupied with reading until the second hour, [2] provided that there be no necessity for something to be done in common, at which time the reading is then omitted. [3] After the second hour, let each one be ready at his task until the ninth hour; [4] let him complete *without murmuring* (Phil 2:14) what has been enjoined upon him.

Chapter 6

[1] At the hour of prayer, when the signal has been given, [2] let him who has not immediately set aside any task that he is doing and is not ready (since nothing ought to come before prayer) be reproached by the abbot or the prior; [3] and unless he asks forgiveness while prostrate on the floor, let him be excommunicated.

Chapter 7

But let no one speak, especially at table, except the one who presides or whoever has been asked.

VIII. [1] Ad necessaria quaerenda in cellula, bini egrediantur vel terni fratres: [2] et ita illi, quibus creditur, [3] non qui verbositatem aut gulam sectantur.

IX. [1] Si quis vero extra conscientiam abbatis vel praepositi, qualemcumque locum egressus, gulae vel ebrietati se sociaverit; [2] aut si in proximo transmissus, pro sua levitate vel gula, non statim expedita necessitate ad cellam redierit, [3] cum in id facinus fuerit detectus, ut canones docent, aut triginta diebus a communione separetur, aut virgis caesus emendetur.

X. [1] Quod si casu quis frater de cellula ex qualibet scandali causa exire voluerit, [2] nihil penitus nisi nugalissimo induatur vestimento, [3] et extra communionem infidelis discedat.

XI. [1] Illud quoque statuimus ut abbates omni tempore cum fratribus reficiant: [2] quia eo tempore quo fratres aut pro negligentia arguere, aut spiritali debent sermone imbuere, absque certa necessitate se removere non debent.

XII. [1] Id etiam pro custodienda fama specialiter statuimus, [2] ut nullus monachus in infirmitate positus relicto monasterio parentum suorum studio commendetur: [3] quia magis cum saecularium spectaculorum visu aut auditu pollui censemus, quam ab aegritudine posse purgari.

8.0 RMac 22; perhaps this serves as an introduction to the chapter that follows and that expands on the same subject.

9.3 According to Mundó, p. 120, n. 35, this is a reference to ch. XLI of the Council of Agde (PL 84, col. 269).

10.0 RMac 28.1-3.

11.1-2 This injunction modifies RIVP 2.41; cf. RB 53.16; 56.

Chapter 8

[1] When necessities are sought for the cell, let the brothers go out by two's or three's; [2] and let them be such who are trusted, [3] not who follow gossip or their appetite.

Chapter 9

[1] If anyone should go anywhere without the knowledge of the abbot or prior and associates himself with others in gluttony and drunkenness; [2] or if he is sent out into the neighborhood and does not return to the cell immediately after the errand has been completed on account of his irresponsibility and gluttony, [3] when he has been found out in this sin, let him be separated from the community for thirty days or let him be corrected with the rod, as the canons teach.

Chapter 10

[1] And if perchance a brother wants to leave the cell for some reason of contention, [2] let him wear nothing except the most ragged clothes, [3] and let him depart as a faithless one outside the community.

Chapter 11

[1] This also we established, that the abbots should always eat with the brothers; [2] for they must not absent themselves without absolute necessity at that time, when they must reprove the brothers because of laxness or encourage them with spiritual words.

Chapter 12

[1] This also we established especially for the preservation of reputation, [2] that no monk who is sick should on that account leave the monastery to be entrusted to the care of his family, [3] because we believe that he can be more polluted than cured of his illness by sights and sounds of the secular world.

XIII. [1] Si quis vero monachus furtum fecerit, quod potius sacrilegium dici potest, [2] id censuimus ordinandum, [3] ut iunior virgis caesus tanti criminis reus nunquam officium clericatus excipiat; [4] si vero iam clericus in id facinus fuerit deprehensus, nominis ipsius dignitate privetur: [5] cui sufficere potest pro actus sui levitate, impleta poenitentiae satisfactione communio.

XIV. [1] Monachum nisi abbatis sui aut permissu aut voluntate ad aliud monasterium commigrantem, nullus abbas aut suscipere, aut retinere praesumat. [2] Quod si ad districtiorem regulam non pro actus sui levitate tendentem abbas suus ipsum ad alterum monasterium transire permiserit, [3] ut inde postea sub aliqua occasione egredi praesumat, nulla ratione permittimus. [4] Sane si quis post hanc diligentissimam sanctionem, non observare quae sunt superius comprehensa, praesumpserit, [5] reum se divinitatis pariter et fraternitatis iudicio futurum esse cognoscat.

13.5 "communion" (*communio*): the sense is that a cleric who commits a theft may not be the celebrant at the Eucharist but may receive communion after penance; cf. the Council of Orléans, ch. IX (PL 84, col. 280).

14.0 RIVP 4.1-13 is also concerned with monastic brothers who wish to join monasteries other than their own.

14.1 This repeats verbatim an injunction of the Council of Agde, ch. XXVII (PL 84, col. 267); see Mundó, p. 120, n. 35.

Chapter 13

[1] When a monk commits a theft, which might better be called a sacrilege, [2] we believe this must be followed: [3] if he is a junior, he should be beaten with the rod and never receive the office of cleric, having been guilty of so great a crime; [4] if indeed he is already a cleric when he has been caught in this crime, let him be deprived of that very title; [5] after the satisfaction of penance has been fulfilled, communion alone will be sufficient for him because of the irresponsibility of his action.

Chapter 14

[1] Let no abbot presume to receive or retain a monk transferring from another monastery without his abbot's permission or command. [2] If his abbot has allowed him to move to another monastery because he is striving toward a stricter rule and not because of the levity of his actions, [3] we do not permit, under any circumstance, that he later leave when some occasion arises. [4] Truly, if someone, after this most diligent injunction, should presume not to observe these things that are gathered above, [5] let him be aware that he shall be guilty both before the divinity and the brotherhood.

INCIPIT REGULA ORIENTALIS

I. [1] Ut neque seniores in regendis fratribus inaniter laborent, neque disciplina iuniorum vacillet, quae abbatis conversatione stabilita firma sit, [2] oportet abbatem inreprehensibilem esse, severum, patientem, ieiunum, pium, humilem, [3] ut doctoris et patris locum impleat, seipsum formam praebens bonorum operum. [4] Ad cuius ordinationem omnes fratres respiciant, nihil sine consilio et auctoritate ipsius facientes. [5] Qui sustinens monasterii necessitates, de omnibus quae in monasterio sunt libere iudicabit, [6] nullius personam accipiens nec ulli gratiam praestans, [7] sed unumquemque secundum merita cotidianae conversationis in veritate iudicans, admoneat, hortetur, castiget, condemnet; [8] vel suscipiat, si ita utile videtur, venientes ad monasterium, [9] vel eiiciat, si ita necessitas fuerit, male habitantes.

II. [1] In monasterio seniores sint duo, ad quos vel praesente abbate vel absente omnium fratrum disciplina et omnis cura monasterii pertineat, [2] dantibus sibi vices per dies et dividentibus inter se pondus ac necessitatem monasterii. [3] Ex quibus unus tempore suo praesens in monasterio semper erit, ad praestandum abbati solatium vel obsequium advenientibus fratribus, [4] et ad procedendum, ubi necessitas communis exegerit, atque diligentiam circa omnia quae ad cotidianam custodiam et conversationem monasterii pertinent adhibendam, [5] ut quaecumque ad obsequium usumque monasterii facienda sunt, sine neglegentia et querela faciant. [6] Alius cum fratribus erit, tempore

---

1.1 Cf. 2RP 3.
"abbot's way of life" (abbatis conversatione): cf. RIVP Pr 3; RB 58.17. In RO the term "manner/way of life" (conversatio) is used with regard to the abbot, the monks, and the monastery as a whole.
1.2 Cf. 1 Tim 3:2-3; this scriptural passage is alluded to in RB 31.1; 64.9.
1.3 Cf. Titus 2:7.
1.4 Cf. RIVP 1.10-11.
1.6-7 Cf. RIVP 5.11-14; RB 2.16-22, 23-25.
1.7 Cf. RB 2.22.

REGULA ORIENTALIS

Chapter 1

[1] In order that neither the seniors labor in vain in guiding the brothers nor the discipline of the juniors, made secure and strengthened by the abbot's way of life, vacillate, [2] it is necessary that the abbot be blameless, austere, patient, one who fasts, pious, and humble. [3] Thus he may fulfill the position of teacher and father, himself showing forth the beauty of good works. [4] Let all the brothers look to his governance, doing nothing without his advice and decision. [5] The abbot, who looks after the needs of the monastery, shall freely make decisions on all matters within the monastery. [6] Showing favoritism to no one nor being partial to anyone, [7] but judging in truth each one according to the merits of his daily way of life, let him admonish, exhort, reprove, and condemn. [8] Let him receive, as seems expedient, those coming into the monastery, [9] or expel, if it becomes necessary, those who live wickedly.

Chapter 2

[1] Let there be two seniors in the monastery who will have charge of the discipline of all the brothers and the entire care of the monastery, whether the abbot is present or not, [2] taking turns for days at a time and dividing between themselves the burden and needs of the monastery. [3] One of them must always be present in the monastery during his turn, assisting the abbot and welcoming arriving brothers, [4] going outside as the common need requires and attending to all things that pertain to the daily care and life of the monastery. [5] Thus, whatever things must be done for the care and discipline of the monastery will be done without negligence or complaint. [6] The other will be with

---

2.0 Cf. RPachPrae 115 (CXV). References to Pachomius' Rule are given according to A. Boon's *Pachomiana Latina*: the first notation in each case is to the general section, i.e., to the *Praecepta* (= Prae), *Instituta* (= Inst), *Iudicia* (= Iud), or *Leges* (= Leg); the Arabic numeral refers to the paragraph within a section. Roman numerals in parentheses belong to the alternative, consecutive numbering of the entire rule.

suo exiturus cum ipsis ad omnia opera et omnem necessitatem, providens ne quid contra disciplinam faciant. [7] Qui considerans omnes actus singulorum, si qua contra rationem facta viderit, vel per se emendet, vel abbati indicet.

III. [1] Ille vero, qui secundum ordinem disciplinae ordinatione abbatis ex consilio et voluntate omnium fratrum fratribus praepositus est, omnem ad se curam de disciplina fratrum et diligentiam monasterii revocabit, [2] habens potestatem abbate absente faciendi omnia quae abbas praesens facit. [3] Ille autem patientiam, mansuetudinem, humilitatem, caritatem, aequitatem sine personarum acceptione habebit, [4] ita agens, ut nec abbati taedium generet, nec fratres intemperantia illius laborent. [5] Haec observabit senior monasterii qui fratribus praepositus est, referens ad abbatem omnia, vel praecipue illa quae per se non valuerit explicare.

IV. [1] Commendatum aliquid etiam a germano fratre nullus accipiat.

[2] Nihil in cella sua, absque praepositi iussione, quispiam habeat, nec poma quidem vilissima et cetera huiuscemodi.

V. Operantes vero fratres nihil loquantur saeculare, sed aut meditentur ea quae sancta sunt, aut certe silebunt.

VI. Qui autem coquinat, antequam fratres reficiant, non gustabit quicquam.

2.7 "rule" (*rationem*): this term is similar in meaning to the less technical understanding of *regula*; see notes on RIVP Pr 3; 1.7.

3.0 This chapter, original to RO, describes the office of the prior (*praepositus*) in the modern sense of the term, as the one second to the abbot, but the term itself, in this instance, is still a participial expression: "who is set in charge over the brothers" (*fratribus praepositus est*) and is not strictly speaking a title yet; see de Vogüé, "La *Regula Orientalis*," p. 253 n.

In the later chapters of RO (4, 9, 17, 20, 21, 39), which are taken directly from Pachomius, *praepositus* originally referred to the superior of one of several houses that made up the cenobium and had the sense of "housemaster"; see the translations of the Pachomian rules in Armand Veilleux, *Pachomian Koinonia* 2, Cistercian Studies Series, no. 46 (Kalamazoo, Mich.: Cistercian Publications, 1981). We thank Father Veilleux for kindly providing us with a copy of his translations before their publication.

3.1 Cf. RB 65.14-15.
3.3-4 2RP 5-6; cf. 1 Tim 6:11; Eph 4:2.
4.0 RPachPrae 113-14 (CXIII-CXIV).
5.0 RPachPrae 60 (LX); cf. 2RP 11.
"recite things that are holy" (*meditentur ea quae sancta sunt*): this refers to the

the brothers during his turn, going forth with them to all work and all necessary duties, seeing to it that they do nothing contrary to discipline. [7] If he, surveying the actions of each one, sees deeds in any way contrary to the rule, let him either correct these things himself or let him make them known to the abbot.

Chapter 3

[1] That man who, according to the established order, is set in charge over the brothers by the abbot on the basis of the advice and wishes of all the brothers shall refer to himself all concern for the discipline of the brothers and the care of the monastery, [2] having the power, while the abbot is absent, of doing all the things that the abbot himself does when present. [3] Moreover, he shall have patience, gentleness, humility, charity, equity, showing favoritism to no one; [4] in this way, he will neither be a bother to the abbot nor will the brothers suffer from his own intemperance. [5] The senior of the monastery who is set in charge over the brothers shall be mindful of these things, reporting all things to the abbot, especially those that he is not able to settle himself.

Chapter 4

[1] No one may accept anything given to him, even by his blood brother. [2] No one may have anything in his cell except by permission of the prior, not even the most paltry fruit and other things of that sort.

Chapter 5

The brothers may speak of nothing worldly when working, but let them either recite things that are holy, or surely let them be silent.

Chapter 6

He who cooks, furthermore, shall not taste anything before the brothers eat.

---

ancient practice of "meditation," which was the repetition aloud of memorized Scripture texts while performing some type of physical activity.
   6.0 RPachPrae 74 (LXXVI).

VII. Nemo in cella et in domo sua habeat quicquam praeter ea quae in communi monasterii lege praecepta sunt.

VIII. [1] Cumque ad dormiendum se collocaverint, alter alteri non loquatur. [2] Cellam alterius, nisi prius ad ostium percutiat, introire non audeat.

IX. [1] Mutare de his quae a praeposito acceperit cum altero non audebit; [2] nec accipiat melius et dabit deterius, aut e contrario dans melius et deterius accipiens. [3] Nemo ab altero accipiat quippiam, nisi praepositus iusserit.

X. Clausa cella nullus dormiat, nec habeat cubiculum quod claudi possit, nisi forte aetati alicuius vel infirmitati pater monasterii concesserit.

XI. [1] Nemo a terra solvat funiculum absque iussione patris. [2] Qui in collecta fratrum invenerit quippiam, suspendat, ut tollat qui cognoverit.

XII. [1] Ad collectam, et ad psallendum, nullus sibi occasiones inveniat quibus quasi ire non possit.

[2] Et si in monasterio, vel in agro, aut in itinere, aut in quolibet ministerio fuerit, orandi et psallendi tempus non praetermittat.

7.0 RPachPrae 81 (LXXXI).
"by the common law of the monastery" (*in communi monasterii lege*): the Pachomian text reads instead: "in common by the law of the monastery" (*in commune monasterii lege*).
8.0 RPachPrae 88-89 (LXXXVIII-LXXXIX).
9.1-2 RPachPrae 98 (XCVII).
9.3 RPachPrae 106 (CVI).
10.0 RPachPrae 107 (CVII).
11.1 RPachPrae 118 (CXVIII); taken out of its original Pachomian context, the meaning of this sentence in RO is unclear. Pachomius deals with boats used for crossing the river, where the "rope" (*funiculum*) is used to moor the boat to shore. Crossing the river required a superior's permission, so no one could unmoor a boat by untying its rope from the ground without an order from the superior.
11.2 RPachPrae 132 (CXXXII).
12.0 RPachPrae 141-142 (CXLI-CXLII); cf. 2RP 31-35; 3RP 6.

Chapter 7

No one may have anything in his cell or in his house except those things that are prescribed by the common law of the monastery.

Chapter 8

[1] Whenever they lie down to sleep, no one may speak to another. [2] Let a brother not venture to enter another's cell unless he first knocks on the door.

Chapter 9

[1] A brother shall not venture to exchange with another any of those things that he has received from the prior. [2] Neither may he receive something better and give something meaner, nor, on the contrary, give something better and receive something meaner. [3] No one may accept anything from another unless the prior has given permission.

Chapter 10

No one may sleep in a locked cell nor have a place for sleeping that can be locked unless the father of the monastery has allowed this because of someone's age or infirmity.

Chapter 11

[1] No one may unfasten a rope from the ground without an order from the father. [2] In the assembly of the brothers, let him who has found something hang it up, so that he who recognizes it may take it.

Chapter 12

[1] Let no one contrive for himself pretexts by which he would not be able to go to the assembly or to psalmody. [2] But in the monastery, in the field, on a journey, or in any sort of work, let him not neglect the time for prayer and psalmody.

XIII. [1] Qui minister est habeat studium ne quid operis pereat in monasterio, in qualicumque omnino arte quae exercetur a fratribus. [2] Si quid perierit, et per neglegentiam fuerit dissipatum, increpetur a patre minister operum, [3] et ipse iterum increpet alium qui opus perdiderit, dumtaxat iuxta voluntatem et praesentiam principis; [4] absque quo nullus increpandi fratrem habebit potestatem.

XIV. Si inventus fuerit unus e fratribus aliquid per contentionem agens, vel contradicens maioris imperio, increpabitur iuxta mensuram peccati sui.

XV. [1] Qui mentitur, aut odio quemquam habere fuerit deprehensus, aut inoboediens, aut plus ioco quam honestum est deditus, aut otiosus, aut dure respondens, aut habens consuetudinem fratribus detrahendi vel his qui foris sunt, [2] et omnino quicquid contra regulam scripturarum est et monasterii disciplinam, et audierit pater monasterii, vindicabit iuxta mensuram opusque peccati.

XVI. [1] Si omnes fratres viderint praepositum nimium neglegentem, aut dure increpantem fratres, et mensuram monasterii excedentem, referant hoc patri, et ab eo increpetur. [2] Ipse autem praepositus nihil faciat nisi quod pater iusserit, maxime in re nova. Quae ex more descendit servabit regulam monasterii.

XVII. [1] Praepositus vero non inebrietur, [2] nec sedeat in humilioribus locis. [3] Ne rumpat vincula quae Deus in caelo condidit, ut observetur in terris. [4] Ne lugeat in die festo Domini Sal-

---

13.0 RPachInst 5 (CXLVII).

13.3 "superior's" (*principis*): this is the only place in RO where this older title for the abbot is used.

14.0 RPachInst 9 (CL).

15.0 RPachInst 10 (CLI).

16.0 RPachInst 17 (CLVIII).

16.2 The Rule of Pachomius reads differently: "For in those things which come down from custom, he shall keep the rules of the monastery" (*nam in ea quae ex more descendit servabit regulas monasterii*).

17.0 RPachInst 18 (CLIX).

17.1 Cf. Eph 5:18; Sir 19:2; Prov 23:31. The passage from Sirach alluded to here is quoted by RB 40.7.

Chapter 13

[1] Let him who is supervisor have zeal so that nothing in the monastery is ruined in any occupation that is carried out by the brothers whatsoever. [2] If something is ruined and through negligence is destroyed, the supervisor of the brothers' work will be rebuked by the father. [3] He himself, in turn, will rebuke the other who ruined it, but only according to the superior's will and provided he is present, [4] without whom no one will have the power of rebuking a brother.

Chapter 14

If one of the brothers is found doing something through contentiousness or objecting to the command of a superior, let him be rebuked according to the measure of his sin.

Chapter 15

[1] He who lies, or is detected holding animosity towards someone, or is disobedient, or is given more to joking than is respectable, or is idle, or answers gruffly, or is accustomed to disparaging his brothers or those who are outside, [2] and does whatever is contrary to the rule of the Scriptures and the discipline of the monastery—on hearing about this, the father of the monastery shall punish him according to the measure and result of the sin.

Chapter 16

[1] If all the brothers see the prior too negligent or rebuking the brothers harshly and exceeding the practice of the monastery, let them report this to the father, and let the prior be rebuked by him. [2] Let the prior do nothing, moreover, except what the father has commanded, especially in unprecedented matters. He shall keep the rule of the monastery, which comes down from custom.

Chapter 17

[1] Let the prior not be puffed up, [2] nor let him take a humbler place. [3] Let him not sunder those chains that God joined together in heaven to be heeded on earth. [4] Let him not be sad

vatoris. ⁵ Dominetur carni suae iuxta mensuram sanctorum.
⁶ Non inveniatur in excelsis cubilibus, imitans morem genti-
lium. ⁷ Non sit duplicis fidei. ⁸ Non sequatur cordis sui cogitationes sed legem Dei. ⁹ Non resistat sublimioribus tumenti animo potestatibus. ¹⁰ Ne fremat neque hinniat iratus super humi-
liores, ¹¹ neque transferat terminos regulae. ¹² Non sit
fraudulentus, neque in cogitationibus verset dolos; ¹³ nec neglegat peccatum animae suae; ¹⁴ nec vincatur carnis luxuria. ¹⁵ Non
ambulet neglegenter. ¹⁶ Non loquatur verbum otiosum. ¹⁷ Non
ponat scandalum ante pedes caeci. ¹⁸ Non doceat voluntatem
animam suam. ¹⁹ Non resolvatur risu stultorum ac ioco. ²⁰ Non
capiatur cor eius ab his qui inepta loquuntur et dulcia. ²¹ Non
vincatur muneribus. ²² Non parvulorum sermone ducatur.
²³ Non deficiat in tribulatione. ²⁴ Non timeat mortem sed Deum.
²⁵ Non praevaricator sit propter imminentem timorem. ²⁶ Non
relinquat verum lumen propter modicos cibos. ²⁷ Non nutet ac
fluctuet in operibus suis. ²⁸ Non mutet sententiam sed firmus sit
solidique decreti, iustus, cuncta considerans, iudicans in veritate absque appetitu gloriae, manifestus Deo et hominibus, et a
fraude procul. ²⁹ Nec ignoret conversationem sanctorum, nec ad
eorum scientiam caecus existat. ³⁰ Nulli noceat per superbiam,
³¹ nec sequatur concupiscentias oculorum. ³² Veritatem numquam praetereat. ³³ Oderit iniustitiam. ³⁴ Secundum personam
numquam iudicet pro muneribus, ³⁵ nec condemnet animam
innocentem per superbiam. ³⁶ Non rideat inter pueros. ³⁷ Non
deserat veritatem timore superatus. ³⁸ Non despiciat eos qui
indigent misericordiam.

    ³⁹ Ne deserat iustitiam propter lassitudinem. ⁴⁰ Ne perdat ani-

---

17.5 Cf. Rom 8:13.
17.6 Cf. Luke 14:8.
17.9 Cf. Rom 13:1.
17.11 Cf. Deut 27:17; Prov 22:28; 23:10.
17.12 Cf. Prov 12:20. This scriptural passage is alluded to also in RB 4.24.
17.14 Cf. Gal 5:19.
17.16 Cf. Matt 12:36.
17.17 Cf. Lev 19:14.
17.19 Cf. Prov 10:23.
17.20 Cf. Rom 16:18.
17.21 Cf. Exod 23:8.
17.23 Cf. 2 Cor 4:8.

on the festal day of the Lord Savior. [5] Let him be master of his own flesh, in like measure to the saints. [6] Let him not be found in lofty beds, imitating the way of the Gentiles. [7] Let him not be of duplicitous faith. [8] Let him not follow the thoughts of his heart but the law of God. [9] Let him not oppose higher authorities with an inflated soul. [10] Let him not grumble or snarl angrily against the lowly [11] nor change the limits of the rule. [12] Let him not be deceitful, nor let him ponder deceit in his thoughts. [13] Let him not pass over the sin of his own soul [14] nor be conquered by the lust of the flesh. [15] Let him not wander about carelessly. [16] Let him not speak an idle word. [17] Let him not place a stumbling block before the feet of the blind. [18] Let him not teach willfulness to his own soul. [19] Let him not be unsettled by the laughter and joking of fools. [20] Let his heart not be taken by those who say silly and flattering things. [21] Let him not be conquered through gifts. [22] Let him not be led on by the talk of children. [23] Let him not grow faint in tribulation. [24] Let him not fear death but God. [25] Let him not prevaricate because of fear hanging over him. [26] Let him not abandon the true light for the sake of a little food. [27] Let him not waver or vacillate in his deeds. [28] Let him not change his word, but let him be firm and of determined principles: just, taking all things into account, judging in truth without craving for glory, forthright before God and men, and far removed from deceit. [29] Neither let him be ignorant of the way of life of the saints, nor let him be blind to their knowledge. [30] Let him injure no one through pride. [31] Let him not follow the desires of his eyes. [32] Let him never disregard truth; [33] let him hate injustice. [34] Let him never show favoritism for the sake of reward [35] nor condemn an innocent soul through pride. [36] Let him not laugh among boys. [37] Let him, overcome by fear, not abandon the truth. [38] Let him not disdain those who stand in need of compassion. [39] Let him not abandon justice because of weariness. [40] Let him not lose his

---

17.24 Cf. Matt 10:28.
17.31 Cf. Sir 5:2.
17.34 Cf. Is 5:23.
17.38 Cf. Prov 11:2.
17.40 Cf. Sir 20:22.

mam suam propter verecundiam. [41] Ne respiciat dapes lautioris mensae, [42] nec pulchra vestimenta desideret, [43] nec se neglegat, sed semper diiudicet cogitationes suas. [44] Non inebrietur vino, sed humilitati iunctam habeat veritatem. [45] Quando iudicat, sequatur praecepta maiorum et legem Dei quae in toto orbe praedicata est.

XVIII. [1] Si deprehensus fuerit aliquis e fratribus libenter cum pueris ridere, et ludere, et habere amicitias aetatis infirmae, tertio commoneatur ut recedat ab eorum necessitudine et memor sit honestatis et timoris Dei. [2] Si non cessaverit, corripiatur, ut dignus est, correptione severissima.

XIX. Qui contemnunt praecepta maiorum et regulas monasterii, quae Dei praecepto constitutae sunt, et parvipendunt seniorum consilia, corripiantur iuxta ordinem constitutum, donec corrigantur.

XX. [1] Maiores qui cum fratribus mittuntur foras, quamdiu fuerint, habebunt ius praepositorum, et eorum cuncta regentur arbitrio. [2] Docebunt fratres per constitutos dies, [3] et si forte inter eos ortum fuerit aliquid simultatis, audient iure maiores, et diiudicabunt causam, et digne culpam increpabunt, [4] ut ad imperium eorum statim pacem pleno corde consocient.

XXI. [1] Si quis frater contra praepositum suum habuerit tristitiam, aut ipse praepositus contra fratrem aliquam querimoniam, [2] probatae fratres conversationis et fidei eos audire debent, et diiudicabunt inter eos, [3] si tamen absens est pater monasterii, vel alicubi profectus, et primum quidem expectabunt eum.

17.43 "let him not neglect himself" (*nec se neglegat*): here the Rule of Pachomius reads: "let him not neglect the old men" (*ne senes neglegat*).

17.45 The distinction between "elders" (*maiores*) and "seniors" (*seniores*), as in RO 2.1, is not clear. It is possible the one or other group had some share in the superiors' authority.

18.0 RPachIud 7 (CLXVI).

19.0 RPachIud 8 (CLXVII).

20.0 RPachLeg 13 (CLXXXIX).

20.2 RPachPrae 115 (CXV), Inst 15 (CLVI).

21.0 RPachLeg 14 (CXC).

21.1 "prior" (*praepositum/praepositus*): the author of RO has changed the Pachomian "prior of his house" or "housemaster" (*praepositum domus suae*) simply to "his prior" (*praepositum suum*), which reflects the modern definition of the title (see note on RO 3.0). This change also eliminates the mention of individual houses or hermitages in the monastery; cf. RO 27.

own soul because of timidity. [41] Let him not have his eye on sumptuous banquets, [42] nor let him desire beautiful clothing. [43] Let him not neglect himself, but let him always weigh his thoughts. [44] Let him not be drunk with wine. Let him keep truth joined to humility. [45] Whenever he passes judgment, let him follow the precepts of the elders and the law of God, which has been proclaimed throughout all the earth.

Chapter 18

[1] If one of the brothers has been discovered laughing and playing eagerly with boys, and having friendships with those of tender age, let him be warned three times so that he might withdraw from their intimacy. And let him be mindful of virtue and of the fear of God. [2] If he does not desist, let him be reproved with the most severe reproach, as he is deserving.

Chapter 19

Let those who defy the orders of the elders and the rules of the monastery, which have been established by the precept of God, and give little weight to the advice of the seniors be reproved according to the established order until they are set right.

Chapter 20

[1] Elders who are sent outside with the brothers, for however long they are away, shall have the power of priors, and all things will be conducted by their decision. [2] They will instruct the brothers on the customary days. [3] If, by chance, there arises some contention among them, the elders, by right, will hear and judge the case, and rebuke the fault in a fitting manner [4] so that at once at their command they may make peace wholeheartedly.

Chapter 21

[1] If some brother harbors bitterness against his prior or the prior himself has some complaint against a brother, [2] brothers of a proven way of life and of faith must listen to them, and they will judge between the two [3] if the father of the monastery is absent or has set out for some place. At first they will wait for

⁴ Sin autem diutius viderint foris demorari, tunc audient inter praepositum et fratrem, ne diu suspenso iudicio, tristitia maior oriatur: ⁵ ut et ille qui praepositus est, et ille qui subiectus est, et illi qui audiunt, iuxta timorem Dei cuncta faciant et non dent in ullo occasionem discordiae.

XXII.¹ Nullus mittatur foras ob aliquod negotium solus. ² Missi vero non singuli, sed bini vel terni ambulent, ³ ut dum se invicem custodiunt et consolantur, et seniores eorum de honesta eorum conversatione securi sint, et illi non periclitentur.

⁴ Observantes tamen hoc ut non se invicem fabulis inanibus destruant, neque neglegenti cedant locum destructionis, ⁵ sed unusquisque in actu suo attentus sit, prout tempus fuerit.

XXIII. ¹ Quando autem reversi fuerint in monasterium, si ante ostium viderint aliquem quaerentem suorum adfinium de his qui in monasterio commorantur, non valebunt ire ad eum et nuntiare vel evocare; ² et omnino quicquid foris gesserint, in monasterio narrare non praesumant.

XXIV.¹ Quibus erit potestas legendi usque ad horam tertiam, ² si tamen nulla causa steterit qua necesse sit etiam aliquid fieri. ³ Post horam vero tertiam si quae statuta sunt, sicut scriptum est, vel superbiam, vel neglegentiam, vel desidiam intercedentem non custodierit, ⁴ sciat se cum in hoc errore deprehensus fuerit culpabilem iudicandum, quia per suum errorem et alios in vitium mittit.

XXV. ¹ Cellararii vero cura sit, ut abstinentiam et sobrietatem studens inlata in monasterio ad sumptus fratrum diligenter et

---

22.0 Cf. RMac 22; 3RP 8.
22.1 RPachPrae 56 (LVI).
22.4 Cf. 2RP 11.
23.0 RPachPrae 57 (LVII).
24.1-3 2RP 23-25; cf. RMac 10–11; 3RP 5.
24.3 2RP 4, 35-36; "as it is written" (*sicut scriptum est*): this expression usually refers to the citation of Scripture, as in 2RP 4, but here it refers to the rule.
25.0 Cf. RB 31.1-16.

him; [4] if, however, they see that he tarries there for a longer time, then they will hear the matter between the prior and the brother so that deeper bitterness may not arise because the decision is delayed for a long time. [5] Thus, both the prior and the subject, and those who listen, may do all things according to the fear of God and not give occasion for discord in anything.

Chapter 22

[1] Let no one be sent out on any errand alone. [2] Let those sent out not go out singly, but in two's or three's, [3] so that during that time they may watch and encourage one another, that both their seniors may be assured of their proper way of life and they themselves may not be endangered. [4] Observing this, they may not injure one another with foolish talk nor give occasion to the negligent to cause harm; [5] but let each one be intent upon his own business for as long as the time requires.

Chapter 23

[1] When they return to the monastery, if they should see someone before the gate looking for one of their kin among those in the monastery, they must not go to him and tell him or even call him out. [2] And let them not presume to relate inside the monastery whatever they have done outside.

Chapter 24

[1] The brothers will have the privilege to read until the third hour, [2] as long as no cause arises that will make it necessary that something else be done. [3] After the third hour, if one has not taken care of those things that have been assigned, as it is written, through the interference of pride, negligence, or slothfulness, [4] let him know that when he is discovered to be in this error, he will be judged culpable, because through his own error he sends others into vice.

Chapter 25

[1] Let it be the care of the cellarer, while striving after abstinence and sobriety, to manage faithfully and diligently the

fideliter servet, [2] nihil suscipiens, nec quicquam tradens sine auctoritate vel seniorum consilio. [3] Qui etiam omnia utensilia quae in monasterio sunt, id est vestem, vas, ferramentum, et quicquid usibus cotidianis necessarium est, custodiat; [4] et unamquamque rem proferens, cum fuerit necessarium, ab eo iterum ad reponendum, cui utendo consignaverit, recepturus.

[5] Ad victum vero fratrum proferat ac tradat. [6] Septimanariis ad condiendos cibos det necessaria secundum cotidianae expensae consuetudinem, neque profuse, neque avare, [7] ne vitio ipsius vel monasterii substantia gravetur, vel fratres patiantur iniuriam. [8] Sed et necessitatem infirmorum fratrum ac laborem considerans, nihil aegrotantium desideriis neget ex his quae habuerit, quantum illis necesse fuerit. [9] Advenientibus diversis fratribus escas parabit. [10] Haec erit cura custodis cellararii, recurrens semper ad seniorum consilium et requirens de omnibus, vel praecipue de his quae proprio suo intellectu non potuerit adimplere.

XXVI. [1] Ostiario cura sit, ut omnes advenientes intra ianuas recipiat, [2] dans eis responsum honestum cum humilitate et reverentia, ac statim nuntians vel abbati vel senioribus quis venerit et quid petierit. [3] Nec ullus extraneorum patiatur iniuriam, [4] neque habeat cum aliquo de fratribus necessitatem ac facultatem loquendi, absque conscientia abbatis vel seniorum praesentia. [5] Si quid vero cuicumque de fratribus missum mandatumque fuerit, nihil ad ipsum perveniat priusquam abbati vel senioribus indicetur. [6] Ante omnia ostiarius monasterii haec observabit, ne quemquam de fratribus foris ianuam exire permittat.

XXVII. [1] Si quis accesserit ad ostium monasterii, volens saeculo renuntiare et fratrum adgregari numero, non habeat intrandi libertatem, [2] sed prius nuntietur patri monasterii, et

---

25.4 Cf. RB 35.10-11.
26.1 "porter" (*ostiario*): this term is used in RIVP 4.16 in reference to the minor order by that name; here, however, it has no clerical associations; cf. RB 66.1-5.
26.2 Cf. 2RP 14-15; RB 53.6, 24.
26.4-5 Cf. RB 53.23-24; 54.1-2.
26.4 Cf. RIVP 2.40; 2RP 15-16.
27.0 RPachPrae 49 (XLIX); cf. RMac 23; 3RP 1.

things brought into the monastery for the upkeep of the brothers, [2] receiving nothing nor giving up anything without the consent and counsel of the seniors. [3] Let him take care of all the utensils that are in the monastery, that is, clothing, vessels, tools, and whatever is necessary for daily use, [4] bringing out something when it is needed, and putting it away after receiving it back from him to whose use it had been given.

[5] Let him provide and consign what is necessary for the meals of the brothers. [6] To the weekly servers, let him give what is necessary for providing food according to the allotment of daily expense, neither extravagantly nor miserly, [7] so that from his failure neither the goods of the monastery may be exhausted nor the brothers be harmed. [8] Giving consideration both to the needs and the labor of the weak brothers, let him deny nothing to the wishes of the sick from those things that he has, as much as is necessary for them. [9] Let him provide food for the various brothers as they arrive. [10] Let this be the charge of the keeper of the cellar, consulting always the judgment of the seniors and seeking advice in all matters, especially about those that he is not able to handle through his own understanding.

Chapter 26

[1] Let it be the care of the porter to welcome everyone coming within the gates, [2] giving them a respectful greeting with humility and reverence, and immediately telling either the abbot or the seniors who has come and what he wants. [3] Let no stranger suffer insult, [4] and let no one have justification or opportunity for speaking with any of the brothers without the knowledge of the abbot and the presence of seniors. [5] If a message or anything else is sent to any of the brothers, let it not reach him before the abbot or the seniors have been told. [6] Above all else, the porter of the monastery will observe this: that he not allow any of the brothers to go outside the gate.

Chapter 27

[1] When someone comes to the gate of the monastery wishing to renounce the world and to be added to the number of the brothers, let him not be allowed to enter. [2] But first let him be

manebit paucis diebus foris ante ianuam, ac docebitur orationem dominicam et psalmos quantos potuerit discere, [3] et
diligenter sui experimentum dabit: ne forte mali quippiam fecerit ut turbatus ad horam timore discesserit, aut sub aliqua potestate sit, [4] et utrum possit renuntiare parentibus suis et propriam
contemnere facultatem. [5] Si eum viderint aptum ad omnia, tunc
docebitur ad reliquas monasterii disciplinas, [6] quae facere debeat, quibusque servire, sive in vescendi ordine: [7] ut instructus
atque perfectus in omni opere bono fratribus copuletur.

[8] Haec observabit custos ianuae, referens omnia, sicut superius scriptum est, adnuntians senioribus.

XXVIII. [1] Septimanarii ad cibos parandos vel ad luminaria
concinnanda vel ad nitores faciendos, atque quae ad obsequium
usumque monasterii pertinent, semper parati sint. [2] Hos nulla
alia necessitas occupet, sed in hoc studium impendant, ut rem
susceptam utiliter et diligenter impleant. [3] Et si quid forte nes-
ciunt, de his quae agere debent, sine dissimulatione seniores
suos semper interrogent.

XXIX. [1] Hi itaque quibus disciplina vel utilitas vel opinio vel
obsequium monasterii creditur, officia sibi iniuncta fideliter custodiant et impleant. [2] Hos enim errare non decet, qui ad omnes
errores emendandos praepositi sunt. [3] Qui si vel superbia, vel
neglegentia, vel desidia aliqua ex his praetermiserint quae in
regula continentur, [4] per ipsosque destructio esse coeperit, per
quos debet aedificatio crescere, [5] omnibus condemnationibus,
quas regula continet, subiacebunt.

XXX. [1] Inter omnes fratres hoc observabitur, ut oboedientes

---

27.6 The following Pachomian words have been deleted from this section of
RO: "either in the assembly of all the brothers or in the house to which he is
entrusted" (*sive in collecta omnium fratrum sive in domo cui tradendus est*), since
mention of the individual house no longer applies to the monasticism en-
visioned in RO.
29.5 "the rule contains" (*regula continet*): cf. RMac 24.2: "as the rule requires"
(*velut regula continet*).
30.0 2RP 5-6.
30.1 Cf. Matt 5:34.

announced to the father of the monastery and remain for a few days outside before the gate and be taught the Lord's prayer and as many psalms as he is able to learn. [3] And let him diligently give testimony of himself, if by chance he has done something evil and, troubled, had suddenly fled in fear or if he is under some other jurisdiction, [4] and whether he can renounce his family and surrender his rights. [5] If they see him suited for all things, then he will be taught the remaining practices of the monastery: [6] what things he must do, to whom he must be subject, and the regulation concerning meals. [7] Thus, having been instructed and perfected in every good work, let him be joined to the brothers. [8] The keeper of the gate shall obey all these things, referring and reporting all, as is written above, to the seniors.

Chapter 28

[1] Let the weekly servers always be ready to prepare food, to trim the lamps, to clean up, and to do those things that pertain to the service and utility of the monastery. [2] Let no other duties occupy them, but let them expend their zeal in this, that they may profitably and diligently discharge the task undertaken. [3] And if, by chance, they do not know something about those tasks that they must do, let them always, without delay, ask their seniors.

Chapter 29

[1] Let those, therefore, to whom the discipline, benefit, esteem, and service of the monastery are entrusted, faithfully observe and fulfill the duties enjoined upon them. [2] Hence, it is not seemly for them to err who have been charged to correct all errors. [3] If they, either through pride or negligence or slothfulness, overlook some things that are contained in the rule, [4] and through them destruction begins to take place through whom edification ought to arise, [5] they will be placed under all the condemnations that the rule contains.

Chapter 30

[1] Among all the brothers this will be observed: that obeying

senioribus suis et deferentes sibi invicem, habeant patientiam, moderationem, humilitatem, caritatem, pacem sine figmento et mendacio et maledictione et verbositate et iurandi consuetudine, [2] ita ut nemo suum quicquam vindicet, neque ullus aliquid peculiariter usurpet, sed habeant omnia communia.

XXXI. [1] Sine seniorum verbo et auctoritate nullus frater quicquam agat [2] neque accipiat aliquid neque det [3] neque usquam prorsus procedat.

XXXII. [1] Cum vero inventa fuerit culpa, ille qui culpabilis invenitur, corripiatur ab abbate secretius. [2] Quod si non sufficit ad emendationem, corripiatur a paucis senioribus. [3] Qui si nec se emendaverit, castigetur in conspectu omnium. [4] Quod si nec sic emendaverit, excommunicetur et non manducet quicquam. [5] Cui si nec hoc quidem profuerit, in quolibet loco fuerit, postremus inter omnes in psallendi ordine ponatur. [6] Quod si in pravitate perseverat, etiam psallendi ei facultas auferatur. [7] Quem si vel haec confusio non commoverit, abstineatur a conventu fratrum, [8] ita ut nec mensae nec missae intersit, neque cum eo ullus frater de iunioribus colloquatur. [9] Abstinebitur autem tamdiu quamdiu vel qualitas culpae poposcerit secundum abbatis ac seniorum arbitrium, [10] vel se ex corde pro culpa paenitens humiliaverit et veniam erroris sui omnibus praesentibus petierit. [11] Quod si in fratrem peccavit, etiam ab eo fratre veniam petat, cui iniuriam fecit.

XXXIII. [1] Si quis errori eius consenserit, et secundum duritiam illius magis consilium dederit, ut se tardius humiliet, [2] sciat se, cum in hoc errore fuerit deprehensus, simili modo culpabilem iudicandum.

30.2 Cf. RB 33.6.
31.0 2RP 10; cf. RB 33.1-5.
31.1 Cf. RB 67.7.
32.0 Cf. RPachlud 1-16 (CLX-CXVI); 2RP 27-30, 40-46; RMac 12; 3RP 6; RB 23–25.
32.5-6 Cf. 2RP 43-45.
32.9-10 2RP 28.
33.0 2RP 30, 35; cf. RMac 13; RB 26.

their seniors and deferring to one another, they have patience, moderation, humility, charity and peace—without falsehood and hypocrisy, cursing, multiplicity of words, or the taking of an oath. [2] So that no one may himself lay claim to anything nor take possession of anything as his own, let them hold all things in common.

Chapter 31

[1] Let no brother do anything without the consent and approval of the seniors. [2] Let him not receive anything nor give anything [3] nor go anywhere.

Chapter 32

[1] When a fault has been discovered, let him who is found at fault be corrected discreetly by the abbot. [2] But if this is not sufficient for his amendment, let him be corrected by a few seniors. [3] And if he has not amended himself, let him be chastised in front of everybody. [4] But if he will not have amended at this, let him be excommunicated and let him not eat anything. [5] If not even this profits him, let him be placed last after all the rest, regardless of his previous position, in the order of singing the psalms. [6] But if he persists in his perversity, let even the right of singing the psalms be taken from him. [7] If this shame still does not move him, let him be held back from associating with the brothers, [8] so that he may take part neither in meals nor in the office, nor may any of the junior brothers speak with him. [9] He will be so constrained for as long a time as the nature of the fault demands, according to the judgment of the abbot and the seniors, [10] and until he humbles himself, repenting his fault from his heart, and seeks pardon for his errors before all. [11] But if he has sinned against a brother, let him, in addition, seek pardon from that brother whom he has injured.

Chapter 33

[1] If someone concurs with the fault of such a one and has encouraged him in his obstinacy, so that he is slower to humble himself, [2] let him know that when he has been discovered in this error, he must be judged guilty in like manner.

80   REGULA ORIENTALIS

XXXIV. Hoc etiam addendum fuit ut frater qui pro qualibet culpa arguitur vel increpatur patientiam habeat et non respondeat arguenti se, sed humiliet se in omnibus et emendet.

XXXV. Si vero fuerit aliquis tam durus et tam alienus a timore Domini, ut tot castigationibus et tot remissionibus non emendet, proiiciatur de monasterio, et vel extraneus habeatur, ne vitio ipsius alii periclitentur.

XXXVI. Quod si aliquis locutus fuerit, vel riserit in vescendo, increpetur et agat paenitentiam.

XXXVII. Si quis ad manducandum tardius venerit, absque maioris imperio, similiter agat paenitentiam, aut ad cellam suam ieiunus revertatur.

XXXVIII. [1] Si aliquid necessarium fuerit in mensa, nemo audebit loqui; sed ministrantibus signum soni dabit. [2] Ministri vero, absque his quae in commune fratribus praeparata sunt, nihil aliud comedant, nec mutatos cibos sibi audeant praeparare.

XXXIX. [1] Nemo plus alteri dabit quam alter accepit. [2] Quod si obtenditur infirmitas, praepositus domus perget ad ministros aegrotantium, et his quae necessaria sunt accipiet.

XL. [1] Quando ad ostium monasterii aliqui venerint, si clerici

---

34.0 2RP 40; RMac 16.
35.0 Cf. 2RP 44; RB 28.8; 62.10.
36.0 RPachPrae 31 (XXXI); cf. 2RP 46; RMac 18; 3RP 7.
37.0 RPachPrae 32 (XXXII).
38.0 RPachPrae 33, 35 (XXXIII, XXXV).
39.0 RPachPrae 39-40 (XXXIX-XL); cf. 3RP 12.
40.0 RPachPrae 51 (LI).

Chapter 34

And this must also be added: that a brother who is being accused and rebuked for any fault whatever have patience and not answer back. But let him humble himself in all things and amend.

Chapter 35

When, however, someone is so hard and so estranged from the fear of God that through so many punishments and by so many pardons he does not amend, let him be thrown out of the monastery. And let him be considered just as an outsider so that others may not be endangered by his vice.

Chapter 36

When someone speaks or laughs at table, let him be rebuked and do penance.

Chapter 37

When someone comes late for a meal without permission from an elder, let him likewise do penance, or return to his cell without eating.

Chapter 38

[1] When something is needed at table, let no one presume to speak, but give an audible sign to the servers. [2] Let the servers eat nothing else except those things that have been prepared in common for the brethren, and let them not presume to prepare for themselves different foods.

Chapter 39

[1] No one will give more to another than the other has already received. [2] But if sickness is pleaded, the prior shall go to the servers of the sick and receive what is needed for them.

Chapter 40

[1] When people come to the gate of the monastery, let them be

fuerint aut monachi, maiori honore suscipientur, [2] lavabuntque pedes eorum iuxta evangelii praeceptum, et praebebunt eis omnia quae apta sunt usui monachorum.

XLI. [1] Si quis ad ostium monasterii venerit, dicens velle se videre fratrem suum vel propinquum, ianitor nuntiabit abbati, et permittentem eum accipiet comitem cuius fides probata est, [2] et sic mittetur ad fratrem videndum vel proximum.

XLII. Si propinquus alicuius mortuus fuerit, prosequendi funus non habebit licentiam, nisi pater monasterii praeceperit.

XLIII. Nullus de orto tollat holera, nisi ab ortolano acceperit.

XLIV. [1] Nemo alteri loquatur in tenebris. [2] Nullus in psiatho cum altero dormiat. [3] Manum alterius nemo teneat; sed, sive steterit, sive ambulaverit, sive sederit, uno cubito distet ab altero.

XLV. Si quis tulerit rem non suam, ponetur super humeros eius; et sic agat paenitentiam publice in collecta.

XLVI. Si praepositus iniuste iudicaverit, iniustitiae ab aliis condemnabitur.

40.2 Cf. John 13:14-15.
41.0 RPachPrae 53 (LII).
42.0 RPachPrae 55 (LV).
43.0 RPachPrae 71 (LXXIII).
45.0 RPachInst 8 (CXLIX).
46 "prior" (*praepositus*): it is unclear why the author of RO specifically names the prior, when the original Pachomian text refers more generally to whoever has made an unjust decision.

received with greater honor if they are clerics or monks. [2] The brothers will wash their feet, according to the gospel precept, and will offer them all those things that are appropriate for the use of monks.

Chapter 41

[1] If someone comes to the gate of the monastery saying that he wishes to see his brother or kinsman, the gatekeeper will relate this to the abbot. With the abbot's permission, the gatekeeper will receive the relative after his good faith has been tested, [2] and thus he will be sent to see his brother or kinsman.

Chapter 42

When someone's kinsman dies, a brother will not have permission to attend the funeral unless the father of the monastery allows it.

Chapter 43

No one may take produce from the garden unless he receives it from the gardener.

Chapter 44

[1] No one may speak to another in the dark. [2] No one may sleep with another on the same mat. [3] No one may hold another's hand. But whether standing, walking about, or sitting, let the brothers be one cubit away from each other.

Chapter 45

If someone carries off something not his own, let it be placed on his shoulders, and thus let him do penance publicly in the assembly.

Chapter 46

If the prior has made an unjust decision, he shall be condemned for injustice by the others.

XLVII. Qui consentit peccatis et defendit alium deliquentem, maledictus erit apud Deum et homines, et corripietur increpatione severissima.

---

47 RPachlud 16 (CLXXVI); cf. RMac 13.

Chapter 47

He who concurs with sins and defends another's wrongdoing will be accursed before God and men, and will be rebuked with the most severe reproach.

BIBLIOGRAPHY

Boon, Amand. *Pachomiana Latina.* Louvain: Bibliothèque de la Revue d'histoire ecclésiastique (fasc. 7) 1932.

Clément, J.-M. *Lexique des anciennes règles monastiques occidentales.* 2 vols. Steenbrugge: St. Peter's Abbey, 1978.

Desprez, Vincent. *Règles monastiques d'Occident, IVᵉ–VIᵉ siècle.* Vie Monastique, no. 9. Bégrolles-en-Mauges (Maine-et-Loire): Abbaye de Bellefontaine, 1980.

Fry, Timothy, ed. *RB 1980: The Rule of St. Benedict in Latin and English with Notes.* Collegeville, Minn.: The Liturgical Press, 1981.

Mundó, Ansgar. "Les anciens synodes abbatiaux et les *Regulae SS. Patrum.*" *Studia Anselmiana* 44 (1959) 107–125.

Neufville, Jean. "Les éditeurs des *Regulae Patrum*: Saint Benoît d'Aniane et Lukas Holste." *Revue Bénédictine* 76 (1966) 327–343.

————. "Règle des IV Pères et Seconde Règle des Pères. Texte critique." *Revue Bénédictine* 77 (1967) 47–95.

————. "Sur le texte de la Règle des IV Pères." *Revue Bénédictine* 75 (1965) 307–312.

"The Rule of Four Fathers" and "The Second Rule of the Fathers." Trans. by a Monk of Mount Saviour. Revised and annotated by Adalbert de Vogüé. *Monastic Studies* 12 (1976) 249–263.

The Rule of the Master. Trans. Luke Eberle. Cistercian Studies Series, no. 6. Kalamazoo, Mich.: Cistercian Publications, 1977.

Styblo, Helga. "Die *Regula Macharii.*" *Wiener Studien* 76 (1963) 124–158.

Tertia Patrum Regula ad Monachos. J. P. Migne. *Patrologia Latina* 103, cols. 443–446.

Turbessi, Giuseppe. *Regole monastiche antiche.* Rome: Edizioni Studium, 1974.

Veilleux, Armand. *Pachomian Koinonia 2.* Cistercian Studies Series, no. 46. Kalamazoo, Mich.: Cistercian Publications, 1981.

Verheijen, Luc. *La Règle de Saint Augustin.* 2 vols. Paris: Études Augustiniennes, 1967.

87

de Vogüé, Adalbert. "The Cenobitic Rules of the West." Cistercian Studies 12 (1977) 175–183.

———. *Community and Abbot in the Rule of Saint Benedict.* Trans. Charles Philippi. Cistercian Studies Series, no. 5/1. Kalamazoo, Mich.: Cistercian Publications, 1979.

———. "La *Regula Orientalis*. Texte critique et synopse des sources." *Benedictina* 13:2 (1976) 241–271.

———. "La Vie des Pères du Jura et la datation de la *Regula Orientalis*." *Revue d'ascétique et de mystique* 47 (1971) 121–127.

———. "*Sub regula vel abbate*: A Study of the Theological Significance of the Ancient Monastic Rules." *Rule and Life: An Interdisciplinary Symposium.* Edited by M. B. Pennington. Spencer, Mass.: Cistercian Publications, 1971. Pp. 21–63.